Welsh Fairy Tales, Myths & Legends

With thanks to Carys Glyn for the Welsh titles.

Published in the UK by Scholastic Children's Books, 2021
Euston House, 24 Eversholt Street, London, NW1 1DB, UK
A division of Scholastic Limited.

London – New York – Toronto – Sydney – Auckland
Mexico City – New Delhi – Hong Kong

ISBN 978-93-5471-870-0

A CIP catalogue record for this book is available from the British Library.

www.scholastic.co.uk

This reprint edition September 2024

Printed in India at Shivam Offset Press, New Delhi

Welsh Fairy Tales, Myths & Legends

Claire Fayers

SCHOLASTIC

Contents

The Dragon and the Flag 9
Y Ddraig a'r Faner

Flower-Face 23
Blodeuwedd

My Brother the Fairy 39
Fy Mrawd y Dylwythen Deg

Gelert the Brave 53
Gelert Ddewr

Devil's Bridge 61
Pont y Diafol

Rhiannon and Pwyll 71
Rhiannon a Pwyll

The Boy Who Asked Questions 85
Y Bachgen a Ofynnodd Gwestiynau

The Girl from Llyn-y-Fan-Fach 99
Y Ferch o Lyn-y-Fan-Fach

The Fairy Harp 109
Telyn y Tylwyth Teg

The Leaves That Hung but Never Grew 123
Y Dail a Hongia Heb Dyfu

The Devil and Giant Jack 141
Y Diafol a Jac y Cawr

Rhiannon and her Baby 155
Rhiannon a'i Babi

Tappers in the Copper Mine 163
Pwca yn y Pwll Copr

The Drowned Land 173
Y Wlad o Dan Dŵr

Three Calves 183
Y Tri Llo

Taliesin Saves the Day 195
Taliesin yn Achub y Dydd

Pryderi and the Fairy Queen 209
Pryderi a Brenhines y Tylwyth Teg

The Afanc 223
Yr Afanc

King Arthur's Cave 235
Ogof Brenin Arthur

To the Family Bookworms,
Simon, Zoe, Noah, Nina
and Kit.

Introduction

Wales is often known as the land of song. It is also a land of stories. From legends of King Arthur to tales of the Tylwyth Teg – the Welsh fairy folk who hide in every valley – there are stories for everyone.

One of the things I love about Welsh stories is that so many of them are based on real places. In this book, you'll travel from the Black Mountains of South Wales, where Jack the Giant played cards with the devil, to Cardigan Bay in the north, which was once all dry land. Wherever you tread, you are stepping on stories, and once you know them you will never look at the place in quite the same way again.

The most famous collection of Welsh stories is the Mabinogion. They come from a time of giants and enchanters, when Wales was ruled by kings, princes and lords who were often at war. I've included some of these tales in this collection, but there are many more. I recommend looking up one of the many modern retellings of the Mabinogion if you'd like to read more. There are many versions available.

These are just some of my favourite stories from Wales. I hope you enjoy them as much as I do.

A Guide to Welsh Pronunciation

Welsh words can look a bit terrifying if you're not used to them, but the same letters are usually pronounced the same way so it's quite easy when you're used to it.

Here are the main differences from English:

aw – is pronounced "ow"
ch – is pronounced like the "ch" in "loch"
dd – is like the "th" in "breathe" (and "th" is always a soft sound, like the "th" in "thin")
f – is pronounced like "v"
ff – is pronounced like "f"
ll – is a sound that doesn't exist in English. Touch the tip of your tongue to the roof of your mouth and blow around the sides of it.

rh – is like an “r” but with more air
w – is pronounced like “oo”
y – is pronounced “uh,” “i” or “ee”

A Guide to Pronouncing Welsh Names in the Stories

The Dragon and the Flag

Dinas Emrys – DINas EMris

Flower-Face

Blodeuwedd – BlodAYwith
Lleu Llaw Gyffes – Ll-oo Ll-ow GUF-ess
Gwydion – GWIDee-on
Gronw Pebyr – GRONoo PEBBer

My Brother the Fairy

Tylwyth Teg – TULwith Teg

Devil's Bridge

Mynach – MUNach

Rhiannon

Pwyll – Poy-ll
Gwawl – Gwowl

The Boy Who Asked Questions

Gwion – GWEE-on

The Girl from Llyn-y-Fan Fach

Llyn-y-Fan – Ll-in uh van

Pryderi and the Fairy Queen

Pryderi – Prid-E-ree
Manawydan – Man-ow-i-dan

THE FAIRY HARP

Eisteddfod – Ay-STETH-vod
Ar hyd y Nos – Ar heed uh norse

TAPPERS IN THE MINE

Pwca – Puka (rhymes with Booka)

THE DROWNED LAND

Cantre'r Gwaelod – CAN-trair GWAI-lod

TALIESIN SAVES THE DAY

Elffin – ELphin
Maelgwn – MILE-gon

THE AFANC

Afanc – Avanc

The Dragon and the Flag

Y Ddraig a'r Faner

Have you ever wondered why the Welsh flag has a red dragon on it? The story goes back more than fifteen hundred years, all the way to the fifth century, to the time when Vortigern was King of the Britons.

Vortigern, King of the Britons, was worried. The people of Britain faced a new and fierce enemy called the Saxons. Every week there were new reports of people's homes being attacked, their farms burned, sheep and cows stolen. His people needed a safe place, Vortigern thought: somewhere they could go if they needed to hide. Somewhere his soldiers could rest between battles. In his mind he saw a great fortress with stone walls and iron gates, standing high on a hill.

King Vortigern hurried off to speak to his advisors. They all agreed that a fortress was what they needed, and after a lot of discussion, they chose a hill near Dinas Emrys in North Wales. It was high up, so Vortigern's soldiers would be able to see the Saxons from a long way away; it was surrounded on all sides by forest, which would provide wood for fires; and it was near a lake, so there would be water for drinking and washing

Next, Vortigern called his whole court together and told them about the plan. Everybody cheered to hear the news, and the king commanded the best builders, ironworkers and carpenters in the country to come to Dinas Emrys. They set up a camp beside the lake and then, chattering and laughing in the

Welsh sunshine, which, as everyone knows, is the best kind of sunshine, they set to work.

The first day sped by. Teams of workers cut stone from the nearby mountains and brought it to the camp ready to be built into the fortress. Carpenters cut down trees; ironworkers lit fires. Foundations were dug and the very first stone of the very first wall was set in place. As the sun set, everyone celebrated.

The next morning, they returned to work and found a terrible sight. Broken tools, pieces of wood smashed and thrown everywhere. The foundation stone that had been laid in place so carefully was lying on the grass, broken in two.

There was a moment's horrified silence before everyone started shouting. Who could have done this? It must be the Saxons – they'd come in the night when everyone was sleeping!

King Vortigern made his way to the front of the crowd. He was wondering how the Saxons had managed to destroy a whole day's building work without any of his soldiers hearing a thing. And without leaving a single footprint, he realized, looking at the ground.

"We're not going to let the Saxons beat us," he said. He ordered the builders to start the walls again, and everyone set to work, looking noticeably less happy than on the first day.

They worked all day without a break, and by the time the sun had set they'd built the first metre of wall.

The people were too tired to celebrate that night. Vortigern posted guards to keep watch around the hill and in the forest to wait for the Saxon raiders.

The next morning, the fortress wall was lying in pieces again. The guards, rubbing their eyes sleepily, admitted they must have dozed off because they hadn't seen or heard a thing.

So it went on for a whole week. Every day the builders would work as hard as they could, and every night some invisible enemy threw down the walls. The builders started to whisper that the hill was haunted.

"My king," Vortigern's advisors said. "We advise you to abandon this place and build your fortress somewhere else."

Vortigern shook his head. If he abandoned this hillside, people would say he'd given up. The Saxons would laugh and call him a failure. "We must finish the fortress," he said. "You're supposed to be clever people. You go away and find out what's happening every night and how we can stop it. I will give a hundred pieces of gold to whoever solves this mystery."

Vortigern's advisors withdrew. A week later they came back, all of them looking very worried.

"Do you want the good news, the bad news, or the very bad news?" they asked.

Vortigern sighed. "Just tell me what's wrong and how I can fix it."

The advisors shuffled their feet and whispered to one another.

"The good news is we've found out why your fortress is falling down," they said. "There is a curse on Dinas Emrys. No building will ever stand there. That's the bad news."

Vortigern had never heard of a cursed hill. He didn't know much about curses, but he knew one thing: they could be broken. "Tell me what I have to do," he said.

The advisors all edged backward. One of them put up a hand. "Wouldn't it be better to give up on this fortress idea?"

Of course it wouldn't be. Kings never gave up. Vortigern wasn't going to let the Saxons say he was so weak he couldn't even get his own fortress to stand up. Absolutely not. Vortigern rose to his feet. "I order you to tell me how to break this curse."

The advisors trembled with fear, but as Vortigern had pointed out, they were clever people, and they knew they couldn't disobey an order from the king. "Well, Your Majesty," they said. "That's the very bad news. First, you must find a boy who has never had a father."

"Ridiculous," Vortigern snapped. "All children have fathers."

"Nevertheless," the advisors said. "If you wish to break the curse, that is what you must do. You must find this boy and take him to the top of the hill. And then. . ."

"And then what?" Vortigern demanded.

His advisors all found very interesting things to look at on the floor. "And then, Your Majesty," they mumbled, "you must kill him."

Vortigern fell back into his chair, horrified. "I'm not killing a child."

There had to be some other way to break the curse.

That night, Vortigern climbed the hill alone and sat down in the dark. No one had been here for days and the hillside was littered with bits of broken wood and stones. Vortigern stared down at the forests below and clenched his fists until his nails bit into his palms. He would stay awake all night, he promised. He wouldn't leave this spot until he found out what was happening.

He yawned.

When he woke, it was morning. He was stiff and sore from lying on the ground, and there were even more stones scattered about.

Vortigern stumbled back to the camp, red-faced. "The hill is cursed," he said. "It is impossible to stay awake there."

But he still wasn't ready to give up. He sent messengers out across the country, offering a hundred gold pieces to anyone who could solve the mystery of Dinas Emrys.

A week went by, and then a month, and then a young boy arrived at the king's camp. He looked to be about nine years old. His hair was as black as a raven's wings, and his dark eyes had a strange look to them, as if he was staring straight through you.

Vortigern felt a cold shiver. "Who are you?" he asked. "What's your name? Where do you come from?"

"Your Majesty," the boy said. "I am the boy who never had a father."

Vortigern jumped up in surprise. He hadn't told anyone what his advisors had said. How had the boy found out – and what else did he know?

"I'm not going to kill you," Vortigern said hurriedly.

The boy gave a mysterious smile. "I know. But let me spend tonight on the hill, and tomorrow I'll tell you why your fortress is falling."

Vortigern shook his head. He'd already tried that himself so he knew it wouldn't work. Well, if the boy wanted to spend the night outside, why not let him? He'd be safe enough up there for one night. Besides, there was definitely something strange about him, the king thought. Maybe those piercing eyes would see something that everyone else had missed.

"Very well," Vortigern agreed.

He sent the boy to the hillside, loaded up with blankets and food for the night. Then he ordered his solders to stand guard around the bottom of the hill just in case any Saxons came along.

The next morning, the king woke as soon as it was light. He got dressed quickly and ran all the way up the hill. He'd half expected to find that the boy had run away in the night, but no, he was there.

"Your Majesty," the boy announced. "You were right: there was a curse on Dinas Emrys. A powerful spell that caused anyone on the hill at night to fall asleep. But I have broken the spell and now we can uncover the secret of this place. Call all your builders up here and order them to dig and you'll see what the hill is hiding."

"Can't you just tell me?" Vortigern asked. They'd been trying to build and now the boy wanted them to dig? If they didn't find anything, he was going to be the most unpopular king in the history of Britain. What if the boy was a Saxon spy, sent to waste their time?

"I'm not a Saxon spy," the boy said, though Vortigern hadn't said a word.

That decided the king. He hurried back down to his camp and gave orders for all his builders to set to work digging.

They dug all day, not even stopping to rest, and finally, just as the sun was turning orange in the sky, one of the builders gave a shout. His shovel had driven through the earth and into an empty space below.

Quickly, they widened the hole so Vortigern could see inside.

A cave! There was a great big cave inside the hill. A few stalactites hung down, and far below, Vortigern saw the glint of dark water.

The surface of the underground lake began to churn and bubble. The ground trembled.

Vortigern stumbled back. The builders dropped their spades and ran.

"Stay where you are," the boy commanded, and everyone stopped still, as if it was the king who'd given the order.

The next moment, two shapes burst out of the lake. Winged, scaly, snapping, fire-breathing shapes.

Dragons!

One of the dragons was white, its scales shining like diamonds against the darkness of the cave. The second dragon had scales the colour of rubies and wings that looked like moving sheets of flame. The astonished king watched them fly at each other, snarling and hissing, tumbling together to crash against the cave walls. The white dragon blew out pale blue flame, so hot that Vortigern could feel it from where he was standing. He was sure the red dragon would be burned up, but the creature rolled to one side and met the blue fire with a great gush of blazing scarlet flames.

The air sizzled. Vortigern drew back, feeling his hair starting to singe.

"This is the cause of your trouble, King Vortigern,"

the boy said. "These dragons have been trapped here for a thousand years and every night they wake up and fight. While they are here, your fortress will never stand."

Vortigern watched the dragons fight. All night they fought, while the ground shook and stones from the building site rolled down the hill.

Finally, as day was breaking, the white dragon looked up and seemed to see the hole in the cavern roof for the first time. It beat its wings and soared higher, mouth open ready to breathe out flame. But the red dragon darted in behind and closed its jaws over the white dragon's tail.

The white dragon fell back. It let out an awful scream and tried to shake its enemy off, but the red dragon clung on. They both flew in clumsy circles, the white dragon trying to break free while all the time, the red dragon held on.

Vortigern gripped his sword anxiously. "We should do something."

"Wait," said the boy.

The red dragon swung the white one around and suddenly let go. The white dragon spun into the cavern wall. It bounced off, looking stunned, and then, with a roar of pain, it shot up, out of the hole in the roof, and fled into the sky, where it disappeared from view.

The red dragon roared in triumph and dived into the lake. A moment later, the water was completely still again.

Vortigern scratched his head, feeling dazed. If he hadn't seen the dragons himself, he'd never have believed they were there.

"The red dragon will sleep now," the boy said. "The white dragon is defeated. You can build your fortress in peace."

Vortigern tore his gaze away from the underwater lake to the boy. Once again, he had the uncomfortable feeling that the boy was looking right through him.

"I owe you a hundred pieces of gold," Vortigern said. "What's your name?"

The boy shook his head. "You can keep your gold. I don't need it." He started to walk away, then he stopped and turned back. "My name," he said, "is Merlin."

Merlin grew up to be the most famous magician ever. If you know any of the stories of King Arthur, you'll have heard of him.

Some people say this is only a story. The white dragon,

they say, represented the Saxon people and the victorious red dragon represented the brave Britons.

But there's another story, and this one is definitely real. In 1945, archaeologists were excavating the hillside near Dinas Emrys and they found a cavern with an underground lake and the remains of a fortress which had been rebuilt many times. They didn't find the dragon, though. Maybe it's still sleeping.

Flower-Face

Blodeuwedd

This story comes from a collection of Welsh tales called the Mabinogion. They are set in the distant past, when Wales was a land of magic and danger lurked everywhere. Even flowers, which look so innocent scattered across grassy meadows, might be watching you and plotting murder...

Long ago, when Wales was ruled by princes with strange names, there lived a prince who was called Lleu Llaw Gyffes. Lleu, as well as having a name almost nobody could spell, had magic in his family. His Uncle Gwydion was a sorcerer. Gwydion knew that the world was a dangerous place and he wanted to keep Lleu safe. So, while Lleu was growing up, Gwydion cast a great many enchantments on him to protect him from anything and everything.

Prince Lleu cannot be killed during the day or the night. Prince Lleu cannot be killed indoors or outdoors. Prince Lleu cannot be killed while on foot or on horseback. Prince Lleu cannot be killed while dressed or undressed.

And, just in case . . .

Prince Lleu can only be harmed by a spear that is made over the course of a whole year, on Sundays while everyone else is in church.

Nobody would miss church for a whole year, Gwydion thought. He told Lleu all about the enchantments and warned him not to tell anyone.

"Thanks, Uncle Gwydion," Lleu said, and ran straight off to his friends. "Guess what?" he said. "I'm protected by magic."

Luckily, he stopped before he told everyone what

the exact magic was, but by the time he grew up, everyone knew. Prince Lleu was protected by magic.

There was one other spell that Lleu didn't tell anyone about. This one had been cast by his mother, and Lleu was a bit embarrassed about it. The spell was this: Lleu could never get married to any woman born on Earth. If you want to know how that spell happened, you can find the story in the Mabinogion.

When he was young, Lleu didn't care. But the years passed and his friends got married one by one, he started to feel lonely. And so, one day, he went to ask his Uncle Gwydion for help.

Lleu found the magician sunbathing in the flower-filled meadow outside the castle.

"Uncle Gwydion," Lleu said, "I've decided I want to get married. I need you to make me a wife with magic."

His uncle sat up straight. "That is the silliest idea I've ever heard. What do you want a wife for? Wives are far too clever, and clever people are far too dangerous."

That seemed a pretty silly thing to say, Lleu thought, though he didn't dare repeat it. "Then make me a wife out of something safe." He picked a daisy from the grass and began pulling the petals off one at a time. "She loves me, she loves me not, she loves me, she loves me not . . ."

Gwydion watched him, scowling. "Go home and forget about wives."

Lleu threw the daisy at him. "It's not fair! All my friends are getting married – I don't see why I can't. I order you to make me a wife."

The look on Gwydion's face told Lleu what the magician thought of being ordered about. The prince almost turned and ran back to the castle, but he stamped his feet in the grass and tried to look princely and commanding.

Gwydion stared for a few moments, then he stood up. "All right," he said, "I'll make you a wife, but don't come blaming me when it all goes wrong. Now, help me pick some flowers."

Lleu didn't know why Gwydion wanted flowers. Maybe it was a gift for the magical wife. He started picking: daisies and buttercups, marigolds and cornflowers, even the odd dandelion or two. Gwydion piled them all in a big heap in the middle of the meadow.

"Stand back," he ordered. He waved his hands over the flowers, muttering strange words. Lleu began to feel a bit odd. The flowers shimmered, then swirled up in the air as if they'd been caught by a whirlwind. And then, suddenly, the flowers were gone, and in their place stood the prettiest girl Lleu had ever seen. Her eyes were blue like cornflowers, her hair was the colour of buttercups and her skin was as soft and pale as the petals of a daisy. She wore a long dress the colour of grass.

The girl blinked at them, looking confused.

"Hello," Lleu said, starting forward. "My name is Lleu Llaw Gyffes and I'm a prince. Will you marry me?"

The girl didn't look very impressed. Lleu wondered for a moment if Uncle Gwydion's magic had gone wrong. He looked at his uncle, who was standing with his arms folded and a scowl like thunder. "I did my bit," Gwydion muttered. "If she doesn't like you, it's not my fault."

Of course the girl liked him. He was a prize. Everybody liked him. "You can live in my castle, just over there," he said to the flower girl, pointing. "And you'll be a princess and you can help me tell everyone what to do."

Finally, the girl smiled and nodded.

Lleu was so excited that he didn't notice there was something not altogether friendly in her smile.

"Great!" Lleu said. "What's your name, by the way?"

The girl shrugged. "I don't have one."

What kind of person didn't have a name? "I have to call you something," Lleu said. "You can be Blodeuwedd. It means Flower-Face."

Gwydion carried on grumbling but Lleu ignored him and took Flower-Face back to his castle. They were married the next week and for a while they lived together very happily.

Or, at least, Lleu was happy. Flower-Face liked ordering people about, but she found the castle too dark and cold, and Lleu was kind but he was dull. Sometimes she found herself wishing she could go back to being flowers in the meadow again.

One day, Lleu had to go away to meet with some of the other Welsh princes. Flower-Face would have liked to go too, but Lleu laughed when she asked. "Don't be silly," he said. "Wives stay at home. If I let you come, people will think there's something wrong with me."

Flower-Face knew there was no point arguing with Lleu. He'd never change his mind. She waved him off and then she went back and sat alone in the castle, which felt darker and colder than ever.

One day dragged by, then another, and then, as

evening came, Flower-Face heard hunting horns in the meadow and, looking out of the castle window, she saw men riding by. Visitors! Flower-Face ran outside and waved to them.

"Hello," she said. "I am Princess Flower-Face and I'm married to Prince Lleu Llaw Gyffes. It's getting late. Would you like to come into the castle for the night?"

The man at the front of the group got down off his horse. "I am Gronw Pebyr," he said. "The lord of Penllyn." And then his eyes met Flower-Face's and his cheeks turned scarlet. She felt her own face growing warm too.

Gronw Pebyr and his men stayed at the castle that night, and the night after, and the night after that. In fact, they stayed for two whole weeks, and by the end of that time, he and Flower-Face were in love.

"But what can we do?" Gronw asked as they walked in the castle meadow. "You're already married."

Flower-Face pulled the petals off a buttercup, her face creased in thought. "What if I wasn't married? What if Lleu died?"

"That's impossible. Everyone knows Lleu is protected by magic. He can't be killed," said Gronw.

"'Can't' is such a boring word," Flower-Face replied. "This is what we should do – you go home now before Lleu comes back. I will talk to him and find out how we can kill him, and I'll send you a message as soon as I know the answer."

Gronw didn't want to kill anyone, but he loved Flower-Face and would have done anything for her. The next morning, he called his men and set off back to Penllyn, promising Flower-Face that he'd do whatever she said.

A week later, Lleu came home and found Flower-Face crying.

"I've been so worried," she sobbed. "Every night you were gone, I had dreams that something terrible had happened to you."

Lleu laughed. "You don't need to worry. You remember my Uncle Gwydion, don't you? He cast a whole lot of magic spells on me when I was growing up. I can't be killed."

So Gronw Pebyr was right. Flower-Face wiped her eyes and sniffed prettily. "I don't trust your Uncle Gwydion," she said. "What if he left something out? He's an old man, he might have forgotten something."

"He didn't," Lleu said, offended. "My uncle is the best magician in Wales."

Flower-Face started to cry again. She cried all day and half the night so that Lleu couldn't get a wink of sleep. He heaved a sigh and sat up in bed. "I cannot be killed indoors or outdoors," he said. "I cannot be killed by day or by night. I can't be killed on horseback or on foot, while dressed or undressed. And I can't be harmed by any weapon, except a spear made over a whole year on Sundays while everyone is at church, and no one's going to miss church for a year to make a spear. So, you see, I am perfectly safe and you can stop worrying."

The next day, Flower-Face wrote to Gronw Pebyr and told him everything. *You make the spear,* she wrote, *and I'll take care of the rest.*

She was glad she had a year to plan; it was going to take a lot of work to get around Gwydion's magic. But by the time Gronw wrote to her to tell her he was ready, Flower-Face was ready too.

In the meadow between the castle and the forest, there was a stone as tall and wide as a man. Flower-Face ordered some of the castle servants to build a bathtub close by. She told them to put a little roof over the bath to shelter it, and to get ready to fill the bath with warm water. "And let some of the castle goats into the meadow to graze," she said. "They look hungry."

The servants looked at her oddly, but they did as she asked.

Shortly before sunset, Flower-Face told the servants to fill the bath, and she skipped up to Lleu. "I've got a surprise for you," she said.

Lleu loved surprises. "Ooh, what is it? Tell me."

"You have to come with me," Flower-Face said. She tied a scarf around his eyes and led him out of the castle, across the meadow to the bathtub. So, of course, Lleu didn't see that Gronw Pebyr was hiding behind the stone, holding a spear.

Flower-Face stopped in front of the bathtub and pulled the scarf off Lleu's eyes. Lleu did not look impressed.

"What is this?" he asked.

"It's a bath, silly," Flower-Face said. "You sit in it and watch the sun setting. It's romantic."

"It looks ridiculous," Lleu grumbled.

Flower-Face pouted. "I built it especially for you."

Lleu sighed. "All right. I'll get in. Just don't start crying again."

He got undressed and sat in the bath, the little shelter over his head.

Neither indoors nor outdoors, Flower-Face thought, smiling.

The sun sank lower. *Neither day nor night.*

Lleu shivered. "I'm cold. Can I get out now?"

Flower-Face fetched him a towel to wrap around himself.

Neither dressed nor undressed.

"Wait," she said as Lleu started to step out of the bath. "I've got a funny idea."

"Another one?" Lleu groaned.

Flower-Face laughed at him and ran to get one of the goats. "Stand on the edge of the bath and put one foot on the goat," she said.

Lleu stared at her as if she'd gone mad. "What? Why would I want to stand on a goat? Is this a practical joke? You've got a load of people hiding and they're all going to leap out and shout 'surprise' and laugh at me, aren't they?"

Flower-Face made her eyes fill with tears.

"Oh, all right," Lleu said. "But you'd better not have invited my Uncle Gwydion along. He'll never let me live this down."

He balanced carefully, stretched out one foot and placed it on the goat.

Neither on horseback or on foot.

"Surprise!" Gronw Pebyr shouted. He leaped out from behind the stone and threw the spear.

Lleu tried to dodge aside but he slipped on the goat and fell. The spear went right through his shoulder. Lleu gave an awful cry and turned into an eagle. He flew away, leaving a trail of blood and feathers behind.

"Well, I didn't expect that to happen," Gronw said.

Flower-Face and Gronw went back to the castle and told the servants that Lleu had had a terrible accident getting out of the bath and he was dead. Maybe the servants believed them. Probably they didn't, but no one dared say a word.

One person definitely didn't believe Lleu was dead – Uncle Gwydion. Every day, he went out into the forest to look for his nephew, and one day he saw some feathers on the ground. Looking up, he spotted an eagle perched in a tree. It seemed as if it was half-dead.

"Is that you, Lleu?" he asked.

The eagle turned back into Lleu and fell out of the tree.

Gwydion said nothing to anyone. He carried Lleu to his house in the forest and he looked after him for many months while Lleu gradually regained his strength.

Meanwhile, Flower-Face and Gronw Pebyr lived happily in Lleu's castle and they forgot about

Lleu – until, one day, Flower-Face saw a man riding across the meadow.

Her heart dropped.

"It's Lleu," she cried, running to Gronw. "He's alive."

Gronw grabbed his sword in panic. "What shall we do?"

"You do whatever you like," said Flower-Face. "I'm getting out of here." And she climbed out of the castle window and ran into the forest.

Gronw looked around at the servants, who were all staring at him as if he was a murderer. They were right, he thought. He was a murderer. He should never have listened to Flower-Face. He put his sword down and went to stand at the castle gate.

Lleu Llaw Gyffes rode up.

"I was wrong," Gronw said. "I'm sorry I tried to kill you. Tell me what I can do to make it up to you. I'll give you money, land, horses, whatever you want."

Lleu got down from his horse, and his face was like thunder. "The only thing I want," he said, "is to throw a spear at you, the same as you threw one at me."

Gronw gulped. "Can I at least choose where we stand?"

Lleu nodded.

Shaking with fear, Gronw walked out of the castle and across the meadow to the standing stone. He hid behind it. "Now you stand on the other side," he said. "A nice long way back, if you don't mind."

Surely he'd be safe, Gronw thought.

But Lleu drew his arm back and hurled the spear so hard that it went straight through the stone, and straight through Gronw too, killing him instantly.

That was the end of Gronw Pebyr, but what about Flower-Face?

Gwydion found her hiding in the forest.

She fell to her knees in front of him. "Please don't kill me. You're the one who made me out of flowers, so really this is all your fault."

Gwydion scowled at her, angry because he knew she was half-right. He'd warned Lleu that wives were clever, and clever people were dangerous.

"Don't worry," he said, "I won't kill you." He lifted his hands and muttered magical words. Flower-Face felt herself shrinking. Feathers sprouted from her skin, her arms became wings, her eyes grew big and round. She tried to speak but she could only hoot.

"You'll be an owl for ever," Gwydion said. "You will hide from the sunlight and all the other birds will be afraid of you."

“Hoo,” Flower-Face said. “Hoo-hoo.” And she flew up into a tree to hide.

That is why, if you look closely at an owl, you’ll see that its face is shaped a bit like a flower.

Be very careful of flowers. They may look pretty, but some of them are plotting murder.

My Brother the Fairy

Fy Mrawd y Dylwythen Deg

Wales has many stories of the Fair Folk – the Tylwyth Teg, as they're called in Welsh. They live alongside us humans and most of the time we never know they're there. If you're talking to someone and that person vanishes suddenly, they were probably a Tylwythen. Sometimes the Fair Folk will step in to help people, and sometimes, it seems, they like causing trouble just for the fun of it. Here is one of those stories.

Megan knew all about the Tylwyth Teg. She'd grown up listening to her grandmother's stories about the Fair Folk. They lived in the oak trees in the fields that lay between Gran's cottage and the farm where Meg lived. If you heard a branch rustling at night when there was no wind, that was the Tylwyth Teg. Or maybe you'd be crossing a field under the full moon and for a moment you thought you'd heard voices singing in the distance. You'd better hurry on home and make sure you left a loaf of bread and a jug of milk by the kitchen door, just in case the Fair Folk were hungry.

Be good to the Tylwyth Teg and they'll be good to you, Gran said. *But if you annoy them, even if you don't mean to, you'll be sorry.*

Megan wished her parents would take the warnings more seriously. Mam and Dad laughed every time Gran mentioned the Tylwyth Teg. Silly stories to frighten babies, they said. But Megan wasn't a baby. She was nine, old enough to know that some stories were as true as the ground you stood on. And so she was always careful to ask the oak trees' permission before climbing them, and before she went to bed at night she'd slip into the big old kitchen and put a loaf of bread and a jug of milk on the stone floor by the door. In the morning, the bread was always gone and the jug was empty, which was how she knew the Tylwyth Teg really existed.

Now, Megan had a baby brother. His name was Daniel and he was just six months old. If you asked Megan if she loved her brother, she'd wrinkle her nose at you and tell you not to be embarrassing, but that was only because she did love him, more than anything.

This year had been a busy one on the farm and Megan's job was to help look after Daniel. She was happy to do it. Every morning she'd get up as soon as it was light, take Daniel out of his cot, dress him and take him downstairs, where Mam would give them both breakfast. Then, after breakfast, Mam and Dad would go out to work on the farm and Megan and Daniel would play.

Megan made up all sorts of games. One day they were pirates, the next they were explorers in a jungle, then they'd be flying across the sky.

"You're a good girl, Megan," Mam said when she came back tired and ready for tea. She said it again when Megan helped tuck Daniel into his cot at night.

Megan liked being a good girl.

Harvest time came and Mam and Dad were busier than ever.

"Thank goodness you're such a good girl," Mam said, putting Daniel in Megan's lap. "I know Daniel will be safe with you."

Megan stifled a yawn and smiled.

She spent the day playing and trying to stay awake. Mam and Dad came in late and they both fell asleep in their chairs. Megan put Daniel to bed and then she tiptoed off to bed too.

It was only when she was lying there, warm under her blankets, that she remembered the bread and milk for the Tylwyth Teg. She started to sit up, thinking she should go down to the kitchen straight away, but she was so tired and her blankets were warm. She didn't want to put her feet on the cold floor.

Silly stories to frighten babies, Mam and Dad said. Meg wasn't sure. But even if the Tylwyth Teg were real, surely they'd understand she was tired and they'd let her off just for one night. She'd give them double bread and milk tomorrow to make up for it.

Yes, that's what she'd do, Megan decided, yawning again. She lay back down and within seconds she was fast asleep. She didn't see the shadow that flitted across the window, and she definitely didn't hear the sharp cry of rage that made all the trees outside shiver.

The next morning, Megan woke early as usual, and immediately she felt that something was different. She didn't know what. Her room looked exactly the same. She'd kicked her blanket into a knot in the night, but everything else was in its right place, and when she pulled back the curtains, there were the fields of golden corn and the oak trees gently waving their branches.

She must have imagined it – whatever it was.

Megan got dressed quickly and ran downstairs. Mum was already in the kitchen, feeding Daniel.

"He's hungry today," Mam said, turning her head.

Megan stopped dead. The baby in the high chair looked like Daniel. He had Daniel's round, pink face, Daniel's dark hair, even Daniel's dimply smile. But there was something not quite right about him.

"That's not Daniel," Megan said.

Mam laughed. "What?"

The baby chortled and waved its arms. Megan looked at the spot across the kitchen where the empty plate and empty milk jug should be standing. Something inside her turned as sour as old milk.

The baby laughed.

"Who are you?" Megan asked. "Where's my brother?"

"Can you wait until after breakfast to play games?" Mam asked. "I'm too busy right now. Take over feeding him for me, will you? I've got things to do."

Megan took Daniel's bowl and spoon, and she scooped up a spoonful of soft apple for the baby. He gobbled it down, sucked the end of the spoon and gave Megan a big toothy grin.

Had he grown an extra tooth since yesterday?

Mam and Dad were already getting ready to go out.

"We'll try not to be too late back," Mam said. "You're a good girl, Megan."

Megan didn't feel like a good girl any more.

The day felt longer than a hundred years. Megan barely took her eyes off the baby, hoping he'd do something that would convince her he was her brother – either that, or give himself away as an imposter. He did neither. He looked like Daniel and he acted just like Daniel, except that he seemed hungrier than usual, but that could just be because he was growing.

When Mam and Dad came back, Megan still

wasn't sure. She went to her father, who was scrubbing his hands in the sink upstairs. "Do you think Daniel looks any different?" she asked.

Dad glanced at the baby and shook his head. "No. He's as smiley and happy as ever. It's because he's got such a good big sister."

Megan felt that strange, curdled sensation inside her again.

That night before she went to bed, she put two loaves of bread and two jugs of milk by the kitchen door.

The next morning, the bread was still there and the jug was lying on its side, the milk lying in a white pool. The baby saw it and laughed.

"Something is wrong with the baby," Megan said when Mam came into the kitchen.

Mam frowned. "You're not still playing that game, are you? And you've spilled milk over the floor."

"I didn't spill it," Megan said. "I came downstairs and found it like that. I think it might be the Tylwyth Teg. They're angry because I forgot the bread and milk the other night."

Mam's frown became cross. "There's no such thing as the Tylwyth Teg," she said. "Your grandmother's to blame for this, filling your head with stories. I know you get bored playing with Daniel all day, but we're very busy on the farm and we need you to be a good girl and help."

That wasn't what Megan meant at all. "I like helping," she said. "Daniel is the best baby in the world – but this isn't Daniel."

Mam sighed. "Megan, stop it. There's nothing wrong with the baby, though I'm starting to think there might be something wrong with you to complain like this."

Daniel waved his chubby fists and giggled, and Megan was sure there was a spiteful note in his laughter that she'd never heard before.

For the next two days, Megan watched the baby more closely than ever. He didn't do anything a baby wouldn't do. He ate his food, he crawled, he slept. Sometimes he laughed, and once he cried, when Mam was trying to bathe him.

"It's a phase he's going through," Mam said, rubbing the baby's head with a flannel.

Megan watched from the doorway. Daniel always loved playing in water. Now it seemed he couldn't stand the feel of it on his skin.

Be good to the Tylwyth Teg and they'll be good to you, Gran always said. *But if you annoy them, even if you don't mean to, you'll be sorry.*

Megan wasn't sorry; she was angry. "You're supposed to be the Fair Folk," she said later as the baby lay in his cot. "I forgot the bread and milk one time and you took my brother. That doesn't seem very fair to me."

The baby opened his eyes and stared at her for a moment, and something in his gaze seemed deep, dark and old. But then he giggled and went back to sleep.

Megan slept badly that night. She kept waking, thinking she could hear voices outside.

The next day, she waved Mam and Dad off to work, then she put on her coat, wrapped a blanket around the baby and set off across the fields to visit the one person who might believe her: Gran.

Gran was surprised to see her and even more surprised when, after settling the baby to sleep in the other room, Megan told her everything. The forgotten bread and milk, her strange feeling that the baby was not really her brother but something else, something not even human. How the baby hated water when before he'd loved bath time.

Gran didn't laugh; she didn't tell Megan she was being silly. She listened quietly and, when Megan had finished, she sat back in her armchair, her eyes closed in thought.

"It's rare, but I've heard stories of it happening," she said. "The Tylwyth Teg take a child and leave a fairy in its place. Most people never notice the difference."

"I've noticed," Megan said. "How do I get Daniel back?"

Gran thought a little longer. "The magic of the Tylwyth Teg is all illusion and enchantment," she said. "The truth will break it. That is what you have to do – get the fairy baby to admit what he is."

"But how am I supposed to do that?" Megan asked.

Gran leaned forward and whispered in her ear.

Megan began to smile.

An hour later, she was hurrying back across the fields to her home, carrying the fairy baby in her arms. She didn't even want to think of him as Daniel any longer.

It was nearly teatime by the time she got home. She put the baby straight into his high chair in the kitchen. Then, her heart thudding, she cracked an egg and washed out one half of the shell.

She glanced at the baby and saw that he was watching. *Good*, Megan thought. She took the jar of oatmeal off the shelf and measured one teaspoon of it into the eggshell. She added two teaspoons of milk.

Very carefully, using a cloth to protect her hands, she set the eggshell at the edge of the fire and then she sat and watched, waiting for the milk to bubble.

The baby was still watching, his forehead creased into a big, puzzled frown.

Megan turned away so the baby wouldn't see her smile. Using her cloth, she took the eggshell out of the fireplace and carried it to the back door.

"Mam!" she shouted. "You can tell the farm-workers to come in for their tea. I've made plenty of porridge for everyone."

She heard a sound behind her. The baby was laughing – not a baby laugh but a huge cackle. "Well, I never," he said. "I am older than those oak trees outside, but in all my life I've never seen anything as ridiculous as that."

Megan spun around. "Ha!"

The fairy clapped his hands over his mouth. "I didn't say anything! You imagined it."

"Where's my brother?" Megan demanded.

The baby waved its arms and laughed.

"You can't fool me," Megan said. "Give me my brother back or I'll . . ." She remembered how he cried in the bath. "I'll throw you into the duck pond outside," she said.

The fairy shivered. "Do you have to? I don't like getting wet."

Megan folded her arms. "Give me Daniel back and I promise you'll always have bread and milk."

"Can we have some butter too?" the fairy asked.

"All right. But only sometimes or Mam will notice."

The fairy baby grinned at her and disappeared in a flash of light. Less than a second later, Daniel appeared in his place, unharmed and giggling. Megan picked him up and hugged him.

The door opened. "Where's our porridge?" Mam asked, coming in.

"There isn't any," Megan said. "I was joking."

Mam sighed. "Honestly, Megan, you can be a naughty girl sometimes."

But Megan looked at her baby brother, safe and well in her arms, and she didn't care what anyone thought of her. She knew she was a good big sister, and that was all that mattered.

Gelert the Brave

GELERT DDEWR

Wales is a land full of stories. Happy stories, magical stories, scary stories. Stories to make you laugh and stories to make you cry.

Of all the sad stories, the story of Beddgelert is the very saddest.

Are you ready for it?

Over eight hundred years ago in Wales there lived a prince called Llewelyn. There were two things Llewelyn loved most in all the world: his baby son, Dafydd, and his dog, Gelert.

Gelert was a hunting hound and he was bigger, faster and stronger than any other dog in Wales. His coat was as black as the midnight sky and his amber eyes shone bright with intelligence. Llewelyn said the dog could understand every word he said. Whenever Gelert heard Llewelyn's voice, the dog would jump up, his ears standing straight and his tail wagging so hard people had to jump out of the way.

Every winter, Llewelyn liked to go hunting in the mountains of North Wales. This year was different because Dafydd was only a few months old and Llewelyn wasn't sure how long he'd be away from home. Not wanting to be away from his son for too long, he decided to bring the baby with him.

As usual, Llewelyn and his followers stayed in a small town near Snowdonia and on their first day they got ready early in the morning to ride out hunting. It was a beautiful morning. The horses were stamping their feet, eager to be off; the dogs were barking loudly and getting in everyone's way in their excitement.

Then Llewelyn noticed that Gelert was missing. *Strange*, he thought. Gelert always led the hunting hounds. It wasn't at all like him to be missing.

Worried, Llewelyn went back into the house. He heard servants shouting. Running into the baby's room, Llewelyn found Gelert lying underneath the window, his huge brown eyes fixed on the baby's cradle.

The servants tried to shoo the hound away. Dogs shouldn't be allowed around babies, they said, especially not a dog as big and strong as Gelert. What if he hurt the boy?

Llewelyn laughed. "Gelert is protecting the boy," he said. "He'd never hurt him. Leave him alone."

He went back outside to join his huntsmen. When they returned that evening, Gelert came running out of the house to meet him, jumping up at Llewelyn and licking his hands.

So it continued. Every morning, Llewelyn and his men rode out to hunt, leaving Gelert behind, and every evening, Gelert ran out of the house to greet them as they returned.

After a while, the servants grew used to the dog being in the house. In fact, they decided they liked him being there. The baby rarely cried and everyone knew that he'd be perfectly safe with the great hound watching over him, and so they left him to sleep while they got on with their work.

But then one evening, Llewelyn came back to the house after a long day's riding, and Gelert didn't come to meet him. That was strange indeed. Llewelyn didn't stop to take off his armour or sword, but he hurried straight into the house.

As he neared the baby's bedroom, he heard the most terrible sound. Howling and snarling, and loud thumps as if things were being flung about.

Llewelyn drew his sword and ran the rest of the way to the room, his heart pounding. Flinging open the door, he saw the baby's crib turned upside down in the middle of the room. The fur rugs on the floor were trampled into heaps and Gelert crouched in the middle of them, growling while blood dripped from his jaws.

It felt like the whole world had stopped still. Llewelyn couldn't even feel himself breathe. A dreadful ringing filled his ears and he heard the servants' voices in his head, telling him dogs should not be left with babies, especially not a dog as big and strong as Gelert.

As Llewelyn stood, frozen, Gelert's tail began

to wag, and he bounded across the trampled rugs, maybe to greet the prince, maybe to attack him, Llewelyn didn't know. He couldn't think. He let out an agonized cry, and as Gelert jumped up at him, his arm drew back and he plunged his sword into the dog he loved – the dog that had killed his son.

Gelert fell dead at Llewelyn's feet.

Llewelyn stood, breathing heavily, the sword dropping from his hand. And then, in the silence, he heard a cry coming from underneath the overturned cradle.

His son was alive!

Llewelyn stumbled to the cradle and, barely daring to look, he lifted it up. The baby lay underneath, unharmed.

As Llewelyn bent to pick up the child, he saw something else. Tangled in the furs on the floor lay the body of a grey wolf. It must have climbed in through the window, attracted by the scent of the baby, and Gelert – brave Gelert – had killed it.

Llewelyn's eyes filled with tears. He dropped to his knees next to Gelert. "I'm sorry," he whispered. "I didn't know. I thought you'd . . ." His voice caught in his throat. How could he ever have thought Gelert would hurt the baby?

Trembling, he stood up and laid his son back in the cradle, then he lifted the body of his faithful hound into his arms and carried him outside, where, in a broken voice, he told everyone what had happened.

The people wept. They held a funeral for Gelert, and his story was told again and again. Llewelyn built a memorial in the middle of the town, and he changed the town's name to Beddgelert, which means Gelert's Grave. You can find it there to this day.

It is said that Llewelyn was so heartbroken that he never smiled again.

The Devil's Bridge

Pont y Diafol

Like the story of Beddgelert, this tale stars a dog, but it has a much happier ending. If you are ever lucky enough to visit the village of Pontarfynach in mid-Wales, you'll find some beautiful waterfalls where the River Mynach drops down a narrow ravine. A stone bridge will take you across the ravine. The bridge is known as Devil's Bridge, and this is why.

Patch was a dog, which was, of course, the best thing to be in the world. Humans could keep their two legs and their fingers and thumbs. As far as Patch was concerned, it was far better to have four legs to bound about on, and a good bark to frighten cats.

Patch wasn't the biggest dog around, but he wasn't the smallest either. His coat was an ordinary mix of black and white, and when he became excited – which was a lot of the time – his ears stood up and his wiry tail wagged itself into a blur. He didn't belong to any particular human in the village, but his favourite was a girl called Anna. No matter how busy she was, she'd always find time to stop and play with him, and she'd often sneak him a sausage or a piece of cheese from her shopping basket when no one was looking. She did the same for the other dogs in the village, but Patch liked to think that when she said hello to him, her voice was particularly warm, and she always saved the best bits of sausage for him.

Anna was the youngest human in her family, and her mam and dad seemed to spend half their time telling her to do things and the other half telling her off for not doing them properly. One of her jobs was to look after the cow her family kept for milk. She was a silly creature, the cow, always wandering off and getting lost, and then Anna would be blamed for losing her even though it wasn't her fault at all. It was unfair, Patch thought, and if he ever learned to speak human, he'd be sure to tell her mam and dad what he thought of them being mean like that.

One summer the weather seemed to decide it should be winter already. Every day was cold, and it rained so hard that the streets were full of puddles, and the River Mynach thundered through the ravine next to the village. Patch made himself a little den in the trees by the ravine and he hid to shelter from the rain.

One evening, Patch woke from a nap. He heard rain – obviously – and the louder thunder of the river, but along with them, he heard Anna's voice. Patch scrambled out of his den and shook himself.

Yes, there she was, standing at the edge of the ravine, gazing across. And there, right on the other side, was that silly brown-and-white cow, mooing frantically. Patch had no idea how it could have got over there. It must have walked for miles to find a place where it could cross the river. Either that or it had flown, and Patch was fairly sure cows didn't do that.

Anna looked around as Patch ran up. "What am I

going to do?" she asked. "If I don't get the cow back, I'll be in awful trouble."

Patch didn't see why. It wasn't as if Anna had thrown the cow across the ravine, so it clearly wasn't her fault.

Anna put a foot out over the ravine, as if she was thinking of jumping into the river and swimming across, but she drew back quickly. Very sensible too. She was only a small human. If she jumped into the river, she'd be swept away before you could say "woof".

As Anna stood worrying, a man walked up. He must have walked up because suddenly he was standing right next to her, and Patch knew that people didn't just appear out of thin air. He was dressed smartly in a long coat and a tall hat, like a gentleman, but there was a whiff of strange air about it, a faint smell of burning, even though the rain continued to pour all around. And, Patch noticed, while he and Anna were both soaked through, the strange gentleman didn't appear to be wet at all. The raindrops changed direction when they reached the top of his hat, and they fell all around him but not on him.

"Good evening," the gentleman said, raising his

hat politely. "What appears to be the problem?"

Patch growled. The gentleman frowned and stepped sideways away from him.

"The problem," Anna said suspiciously, "is that, as you can see, I'm here on this side of the river and my family's cow is on the other side. How am I supposed to get her back?"

The strange gentleman laughed. "Is that all? Why, I can build you a bridge across this river right now."

Don't listen to him! It's a trap! Patch barked.

But Anna was looking at the river, her head on one side as if she was thinking. "What kind of bridge?" she asked.

"A stone one," the gentleman said. "One that will last for a hundred years, at least."

Patch tried to bite his ankle. Anna shooed him away. The smell of burning grew stronger, and was that a tail poking out from under the gentleman's jacket?

"And what will you want in return?" Anna asked.

Look! Look – tail! People do not have tails!

The strange gentleman smiled. "I think you'll find the price very reasonable. All I want is the first living soul who crosses the bridge."

Aha! Patch knew this was a trick. The gentleman was not a man at all. He was something older, full of dangerous magic. Patch wouldn't be surprised if he'd put the cow on the other side of the river in the first place.

"Hush, Patch," Anna said. She bent down to scratch his head. Patch usually liked that, but he shook her off and growled at the strange ungentleman again.

They all looked across the rushing river at the cow. Maybe, Patch thought, if he swam across, he could guide her back around to the right side of the ravine? But no, he knew he'd never make it.

"It's a shame, isn't it?" the ungentleman said. "If you try to swim across, you'll be swept away. You'd have to walk upriver to find a crossing place, and by the time you do that, the cow will have wandered off again. You're far better off accepting my offer." He studied his fingernails, which had a few coils of smoke coming off them. "Of course, if you're not interested, I'm sure somebody in your village will be. Maybe your parents would like a bridge?"

"You leave my family alone," Anna snapped.

The ungentleman turned up his collar. "Yes,

come to think of it, maybe you should go home and tell your parents you lost the cow. I'll wait here for them."

Anna's face reddened. The cow started mooing again.

Don't do it! Patch yapped. This wasn't her fault – she hadn't lost the cow. But Anna seemed more worried about her family now.

"If I buy your bridge," Anna said, "will you promise to go away and never come back to Wales?"

The man who was not a man frowned a little and then held out his hand. "You have my word," he said.

He and Anna shook hands, and Patch couldn't do a thing to stop them.

The sky rumbled. Clouds rolled across, thick and dark, and the rain hammered down heavier than ever. Little clouds of steam rose from all the puddles. Patch felt every hair on his body standing on end.

Then stones began to rise out of the river. Lightning flashed and the air became busy with the noise of hammering and strange voices singing. Anna crouched down beside Patch and the two of them trembled.

A few minutes later, the sky cleared, the rain eased, and Patch saw a bridge spanning the ravine. It was made of old grey stone and it looked so solid and sturdy that it could have been there for ever.

The ungentleman straightened his jacket sleeves. "There we are," he said. "One bridge as ordered, all ready for use. I'll just collect my payment now, if you please, and I'll be on my way."

Anna's shoulders drooped. "Sit, Patch," she said.

No! What do you think you're doing?

Anna looked back in the direction of her home.

If the ungentleman took Anna away, there'd be no more scratches on the head, no more best bits of sausage when no one was looking. There'd be no more Anna.

The smell of burning made Patch sneeze. The ungentleman suddenly appeared on the far side of the bridge, even though Patch hadn't seen him walk across.

Anna put one foot on to the bridge and then the other.

Come back! Patch barked, and he ran after her.

Four legs were always faster than two. Patch overtook Anna easily and bounded across the bridge. He jumped up at the ungentleman, yapping angrily, his tail wagging itself into a blur.

There! I'm the first living soul across. Now you'll have to leave Anna alone and take me.

The ungentleman pushed Patch away. "What do I want a dog for?" he shouted. "You tricked me!"

"No, I didn't," Anna said. "Patch did."

The cow mooed and butted at the ungentleman, trying to push him into the river. Maybe the cow wasn't so silly after all. The ungentleman stamped his feet in rage and vanished in a puff of horrid-smelling smoke. But the bridge remained right where it was, spanning the river from side to side, and it is still there to this very day.

As for Anna, Patch and the cow, they hurried home, where Anna told her parents what had happened and that from now on Patch would be living in the house with them and she didn't care whether they liked it or not. But once they'd heard the story and seen the bridge for themselves, they were filled with amazement and delight. They scolded Anna and hugged her and promised that Patch could live with them for ever. Which he did. And he always got the best bits of sausage.

Rhiannon and Pwyll

RHIANNON A PWYLL

This is another story from the Mabinogion, where the Otherworld of magic was never far away.

Pwyll, Prince of Dyfed, was a people person. He hated being on his own, and he was always happiest when he was in the middle of a crowd. He had a company of a hundred knights who were all his best friends, and he never did anything without them.

It was odd, then, that he was feeling bored. He'd been at his castle, feasting all day, and all his friends were still eating and laughing, but Pwyll was no longer hungry, and his friends' jokes didn't seem very funny.

He heaved a sigh. "I want to do something different," he announced. "Something I've never done before."

His friends all laughed and then seemed to realize he was serious. One of the knights got up and pointed out of the palace window. "See that hill up there?" he said. "There's a story that anyone who climbs it will either end up bruised all over as if they've been beaten with sticks, or they'll see something marvellous."

Pwyll had never heard of the story, and he wondered if his friends were making fun of him. If it was a joke, he decided he'd go along with it. "I'm not afraid of a few bruises," he said, "and I'd like to see something marvellous. I'm going to try it."

He left the castle and strode off towards the hill, which turned out to be steeper than it looked. He reached the top and, puffing a bit, he sat down.

As soon as his bottom touched the grass, he saw a lady riding through the meadow below. Pwyll was sure she hadn't been there before. He couldn't see her very well from this distance, but she looked beautiful. She wore a long gold dress, and her horse was so white it almost hurt Pwyll's eyes to look.

He jumped up and, yes, she was still there. Pwyll charged down the hill, waving his arms and nearly falling over his own feet. The lady turned to look at him and then, without a word, she turned her horse around and rode very slowly away.

Pwyll grinned to himself and chased after her. But an odd thing happened. Even though the lady seemed to be riding ever so slowly, he couldn't catch up with her, no matter how fast he ran. In fact, she drew further and further away from him until she vanished in the distance.

Pwyll limped back to his castle, sweating and out of breath, and told his knights what had happened. They laughed and clapped him on the shoulders and told him not to worry. "We'll help you catch the lady tomorrow," they said.

The next day, early in the morning, Pwyll climbed the hill again. This time, all one hundred of his knights waited behind the hill on their horses.

Pwyll sat down on top of the hill. Straight away, the lady appeared.

"There she is!" Pwyll yelled, and his knights all dug their heels into their horses and sprang after her.

The lady glanced up at Pwyll. She looked a bit cross today, he thought, and he wondered why. Then she turned her horse around and rode slowly away with all the knights chasing her. They were galloping, overtaking one another, some of them falling off their horses in their hurry, but the lady ignored them all. Her white horse walked on and, no matter how fast the knights rode, she drew further and further ahead until she disappeared into the distance.

The knights returned to the palace looking shamefaced. "The lady is a mirage," they told Pwyll. "She can't be caught."

Pwyll didn't usually disagree with his friends, but this time he wasn't sure. He'd have one more try, he thought.

He rode out of the castle alone the next morning. His friends would only laugh at him if they knew he was going back to the hill. He rode halfway up the hill, then left his horse and climbed the rest of the way and sat down.

There she was! Riding slowly around the hill, looking up at him from time to time.

Pwyll scrambled down the hill, jumped on his horse and rode after her. Just like the last two days, her horse walked slowly, but no matter how fast Pwyll urged his horse on, he couldn't catch up.

"Hey!" he shouted. "You on the horse."

Actually, that probably sounded a bit rude.

"Um, I mean, excuse me. Would you mind terribly if you slowed down just a little bit?"

And, just like that, the lady stopped her horse. Pwyll was racing so fast he overtook her. He turned his horse and rode back to her, feeling as if he was in a dream.

"Why didn't you stop before?" he asked.

She laughed. "You never asked me to."

Pwyll blushed, glad none of his friends were here to see him. "What's your name?" he asked her. "Why have you been riding here?"

The lady smiled, and Pwyll blushed even harder because she really was very beautiful. "My name is Rhiannon," she said, "and I'm a princess. My father wants me to get married to a man I don't like and so

I ran away. I'm looking for Pwyll, Prince of Dyfed. I've heard he's a great prince."

"But I'm Pwyll!" Pwyll cried.

Rhiannon's eyes sparkled. "Then I have a question for you," she said. She dismounted gracefully and kneeled on one knee in the grass. "Prince Pwyll, will you marry me?"

Pwyll fell off his horse.

Once he'd untangled himself and got back on his feet, he said yes, of course, he would marry her. She was beautiful and magical and she could ride a horse better than any of his knights. In fact, he couldn't wait to tell his knights about her.

Rhiannon shook her head. "You have to keep this a secret," she said. "If anyone finds out, they may tell Lord Gwawl – he's the one I'm supposed to be marrying. The wedding is set for a year tomorrow, so you must come to my father's house in exactly one year's time."

"Why can't we get married straight away?" Pwyll asked.

"Because then my father will disown me and I don't want that." Rhiannon got back on her horse. "One year's time. Don't forget."

Pwyll returned to his castle with the secret

burning inside him. His friends could see that something had happened, and of course it wasn't long before Pwyll had blurted out the whole thing. He told them to keep it a secret and they promised, so he was sure it would be all right.

The year flew by. Almost before Pwyll knew it, it was time to ride to Rhiannon's house. He took all one hundred knights with him, because of course you can't get married without your friends there. The whole company rode up to the doors of Rhiannon's house and Pwyll announced who he was and that he and Rhiannon were engaged to be married.

Rhiannon's father turned beetroot with rage, but with all of Pwyll's knights there he didn't dare say a word. He invited them inside and he gave them a welcome feast. Pwyll sat next to Rhiannon, who was even more beautiful than he remembered, and he grinned with happiness.

Then, just as the feast was finishing, a man walked into the hall. He was tall with brown hair, and he wore expensive clothes and a gold chain around his neck.

"Prince Pwyll," he said. "Congratulations on your engagement. I was hoping you'd share some of your good fortune and grant me a favour."

Rhiannon jabbed Pwyll in the side. "Don't listen to him."

But Pwyll's friends all laughed and cheered and dared Pwyll to say yes, and so he did. "Go on, then," he said. "Tell me what you want and you can have it."

The brown-haired man smirked. "Thank you. My name is Lord Gwawl and I would like to marry Rhiannon."

Pwyll's knights fell silent.

"Pwyll," Rhiannon hissed. "What have you done?"

She dragged Pwyll outside the hall as the feast ended in chaos. "I told you to keep this a secret," she said.

"I did. I only told my friends. One or two of them . . . Or maybe a hundred."

"And they told their friends, who told their friends, until Gwawl heard it. Thanks, Pwyll. Now I'll have to marry him."

Pwyll hung his head, feeling very stupid. "I'm sorry. What can I do to fix this?"

"There may be a way," Rhiannon said. "But this time you have to trust me and not say a word to anyone, not even your friends. Wait here."

She hurried away and came back a few minutes later holding a bag made of strange-looking silver material. "Keep this safe," she said. "I'll tell Gwawl I'll marry him this time next year. Come back then. Disguise yourself as a beggar and beg Gwawl to let you fill your bag with food."

"How's that going to stop you marrying him?" Pwyll asked.

Rhiannon sighed. "Just come back in a year and you'll see. But if you tell anyone and Gwawl finds out, we won't get another chance."

A whole extra year! Pwyll felt as if he was going to burst. He spent the days pacing impatiently around his castle, and whenever his friends asked him what was wrong, he changed the subject.

He'd never done anything without his friends before. What if he couldn't manage it on his own? What if he failed?

But he knew he had to try, otherwise he'd never see Rhiannon again. At the end of the year, Pwyll put a ragged coat over his clothes and rode nervously to Rhiannon's house. He didn't tell a single person where he was going.

Gwawl's welcome feast had already begun. Pwyll could hear the laughing and singing. He slunk into the hall, where Gwawl sat at the head table between Rhiannon and her father. Pwyll's heart lifted when he saw Rhiannon. He wanted to run to her, but he kept his head down. He shuffled into the middle of the hall and bowed low.

"My Lord Gwawl," he said in a quavering voice. "I'm a poor man and I'm very hungry. Please will you let me fill my bag with food?"

Gwawl started to shake his head, then jumped as if Rhiannon had kicked him under the table. Pwyll hoped she had.

"Lord Gwawl," she said. "I thought you were famous for your generosity. Surely you can spare a little food."

Gwawl huffed. "All right, but be quick. I'm about to get married."

They hadn't actually got married yet, then. That was a relief. Pwyll opened his silver bag and began to fill it.

That was when things became strange. First, he put an apple in, then a bread roll, then a whole plate of bread rolls. No matter what Pwyll put in the bag, there still seemed to be plenty of space for more. He added a turkey and a dish of roast potatoes, a ham and a whole trifle from the dessert table.

Pwyll's eyes grew round. Lord Gwawl scowled. "Stop it. You're taking the whole feast."

"You did say I could fill it," Pwyll said innocently.

Rhiannon leaned forward. "Lord Gwawl, this bag comes from the Otherworld. It will never be full until a noble man puts his feet inside it."

"Then give the bag to me," Gwawl shouted. He grabbed the bag from Pwyll's hand, put it on the floor and stepped inside.

Quick as a flash, Pwyll pulled the bag up over Gwawl's head and tied the top.

"Let me out!" Gwawl yelled, falling over. "I'm suffocating!"

Pwyll poked the bag with his foot. "What will you give me if I let you out?"

"Anything you want," the muffled reply came.

Pwyll threw off his ragged disguise. "Then I ask for Rhiannon's hand in marriage."

"And you have to promise not to take revenge for this or to trick me into marrying you again," Rhiannon added quickly.

The bag wriggled furiously. "That's not fair!"

Pwyll gave the bag another kick. "Then you can stay in there. At least you won't get hungry with all that food."

Gwawl struggled and punched at the bag and tried to escape, but the ties on the top wouldn't open. Finally, after a lot of shouting and sulking, he gave up.

"All right," he said. "I promise."

Pwyll untied the bag and Gwawl fell out, covered in bits of roast potato and squashed trifle. He stamped out of the hall and ran home to hide.

Pwyll and Rhiannon got married, there and then. The next day they rode back to Dyfed, where Pwyll told his friends everything and the laughing and the feasting went on for a very long time.

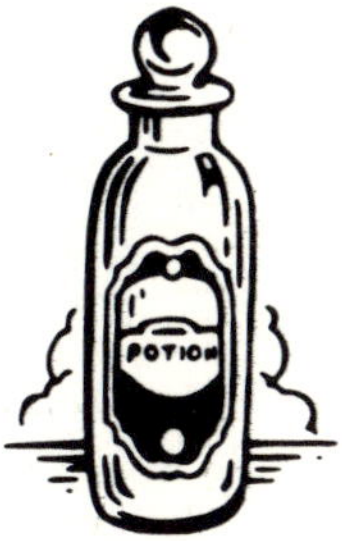

The Boy Who Asked Questions

Y Bachgen a Ofynnodd Gwestiwnau

In Wales, there are many stories about Taliesin. He was the greatest poet, storyteller and musician who ever lived. He sang before lords and princes and kings. He even met King Arthur at Camelot. The stories say that Taliesin knew how to do magic, and before he was born, he outwitted a witch. That story can't be true. How can you do anything before you're born?

Once there was a boy called Gwion, but people called him Gwion Bach because he was so small – *bach* means "little" in Welsh. His parents had died when he was a baby and he didn't have anyone else to look after him, so he spent his days in the town, doing odd jobs for people and asking questions.

Gwion loved questions. Why is the sky blue? What do sheep think about all day? Why does bread rise when you put it in the oven, and why does everyone have to stay away from the big house by the lake?

The answer to the last one was easy. "Because the house belongs to Ceridwen the witch," the baker said, shooing Gwion out of the shop. "If she catches you there, she'll turn you into a frog. Go and play, Gwion Bach, and stop bothering people with your questions."

Gwion wandered off, wondering what it would feel like to be a frog. How was he supposed to learn anything if people wouldn't answer his questions?

He didn't mean to go near the house by the lake. His feet just wandered out of town and Gwion went with them. It was a beautiful spring day and the lake shone as if it had been polished. Gwion wondered if anyone would notice if he jumped in for a quick swim.

Just then, he heard the sound of footsteps and a long skirt swishing through the grass.

It was her! Ceridwen – the witch!

Gwion scuttled behind a bush to hide. Peeking through the leaves, he saw a woman. She was tall and beautiful, but when she happened to glance in Gwion's direction, he felt suddenly unwell, as if someone had grabbed his stomach and was squeezing it hard. He ducked down, his hands clammy.

Ceridwen paused under a tree and picked a white feather out of a bird's nest in the branches. She turned around, frowning as if she was looking for something else.

What was she doing? Gwion forgot to be afraid. He leaned forward, trying to see.

Then – crash! His foot slipped and he fell out of the bush.

Ceridwen spun around. "Who's there?" She strode across the grass and grabbed Gwion by the collar. "What are you doing, little spy?"

Gwion could barely speak for terror. "I'm not a spy. I'm a . . . I'm Gwion Bach." He tried to look as small as his name.

Ceridwen dropped him back into the bush. "Do your parents know you're here?"

Gwion's cheeks turned scarlet. "I don't have any parents."

"You don't?" Something strange flitted across Ceridwen's gaze. Gwion waited, his heart thudding.

"Tell me, Gwion," Ceridwen said at last. "Would you like a job?"

Gwion's heart nearly jumped out of his chest. Him? Work for a witch?

"I'm making a very special potion, you see," Ceridwen continued. "It must be kept bubbling in my cauldron and someone must stir it, very carefully, for a whole year. Do you think you can do that?"

Gwion had stirred mixtures in the baker's shop before, but never for a year. "What if I need the bathroom?" he asked.

Ceridwen laughed. "I have another servant who will help. She'll stir the potion when you need a break – but you'll have to do most of the work yourself. I'll pay you a penny a day and all the food you can eat."

A penny was worth a lot more money in those days. Gwion started to nod, and then stopped, suspicious. "What's this potion for? It's not to turn people into frogs, is it?"

"Do you always ask this many questions?"

Ceridwen said. "No, I don't want to turn people into frogs. The potion is a special potion of knowledge. The person who drinks it at the end of the year will know the answers to all the questions in the world."

A potion of knowledge sounded amazing – and Gwion liked the way Ceridwen had answered his question instead of shooing him away. He stood up straight. "I'll do it," he said. "When do I start?"

The next morning, Gwion knocked on the witch's door.

Ceridwen led him into the kitchen, where an enormous copper cauldron sat over a fire and an old woman in a grey dress and a white apron bustled about.

"This is Gwion," Ceridwen told the woman. "He's in charge of stirring." She fetched Gwion a chair to sit in and took a long wooden spoon off the wall. "Now, remember, you must stir the potion slowly and carefully, and you must not stop."

Gwion looked into the cauldron. The potion swirled with colour. Ceridwen sprinkled in a few golden leaves. "That's the final ingredient," she said. "Now – stir!"

*

For the first few days, Gwion's arms ached horribly and his bottom got pins and needles from sitting still, but he soon grew used to it. Sometimes the servant lady talked to him, and sometimes Ceridwen came into the kitchen and stood with her arms folded, watching, but apart from that, Gwion was left on his own. He passed the time by making up questions. Why did summer come after spring? Where did the birds go in autumn? Why did it only snow in winter?

Once or twice he tried asking Ceridwen some of his questions, but she only told him to mind his own business and keep stirring. She probably didn't know the answers yet, Gwion thought. Once she'd drunk the potion, she'd know everything. He wanted to ask her if there'd be a drop of potion for him, but one look from her cold eyes silenced him. Ceridwen, he thought, would not share her magic with anyone.

One day, the servant lady opened the kitchen door to let some fresh air in and Gwion saw a patch of yellow daffodils breaking through the ground. How did daffodils know it was time to grow? Did flowers have clocks hidden in their leaves?

But then another thought struck him. Daffodils

meant it was spring. He'd been here a whole year. Gwion stirred faster. Soon, he'd be finished. Soon, Ceridwen would pay him and he could go back into town, play in the sunshine and ask all the questions he'd thought of.

He didn't notice that he was splashing the potion – not until three scalding drops jumped out of the cauldron on to his hand.

Ouch! Why did fire make things hot? Gwion stopped stirring and sucked his hand.

His mouth tingled. The drops tasted sweet and spicy and salty and sour all at the same time, as if every flavour in the world had been squashed into them.

And, of course, fire made things hot because fire contained energy. Gwion understood exactly how it worked now. Not only that, he knew why the sky was blue, and how daffodils knew when spring had come. He only had to think a question and the answer was there in his mind.

Gwion looked into the cauldron, where the potion was no longer bubbling. Instead, it had turned to a brown sludge, like mud.

Then Gwion heard Ceridwen coming. He dropped the spoon and ran out of the open door.

A moment later, a terrible cry of rage split the air.

"Gwiiiiiioooooooon Baaaaaaaaach!!!!!"

Ceridwen came charging out of the house like a bull. Gwion sprinted away across the grass, but he'd never been very good at running: his legs were too short and they didn't move fast enough. Soon he was panting, his lungs burning, and he could hear Ceridwen right behind him.

If only he had four legs, like a hare.

At once, he felt himself shrink, leaving his clothes behind, his skin turning to fur, his ears stretching. He nearly fell over his four legs in surprise, but he kept running. The grass blurred beneath him as he raced away toward the lake, his powerful hind legs propelling him on.

But then he heard a dog bark. Gwion looked back and saw that Ceridwen had turned into a greyhound – and she was gaining on him. Across the grass they ran, and though the hare was fast, the hound was faster. Gwion soon felt hot breath on his hind legs.

He couldn't escape the witch on land, but where else could he go?

The lake shone before him. If only he had fins like a fish.

The thought scrambled into his head and Gwion became a silver salmon. His scales tingled as he plunged into the murky water.

Then he heard an angry chirruping. Gwion looked back and saw that the greyhound had become an otter, and the otter dived into the lake after him. Through the water they swam, and though the fish was fast, the otter was faster. Gwion soon felt furry paws snatching at his tail.

He couldn't escape the witch in water, but where else could he go?

He looked up at the sky. If only he had wings like a . . .

Quicker than thought, Gwion became a crow and flapped into the air with a triumphant "Caw!"

The otter shook its furry paws in rage before its fur became feathers, and in a moment the otter was a hawk. It surged into the air, wings spread wide and talons twitching.

Over the fields they flew, and though the crow was fast, the hawk was faster. Gwion soon felt talons grasping at his back.

He couldn't escape the witch in the air, but where else could he go?

There *was* nowhere else.

Ceridwen was faster than him on land, in water, and in the sky.

Maybe, if he couldn't run, he could still hide.

The hawk's shadow fell across him. Its talons snapped down, and as they did, Gwion became a tiny seed of corn. The hawk found itself clutching at nothing, and the seed fell, down and down, all the way to the sandy soil, where it lay out of breath and almost invisible.

Almost but not quite. The hawk's eyes were sharp and they saw where the seed landed. The hawk folded its wings and dropped like a rock, then as its clawed feet touched the ground, it changed into an ordinary black hen.

A hen didn't look very dangerous. The seed lay still, trying not to giggle. Then the hen started to scratch and peck at the ground, and before Gwion could change shape again, she had pecked up the seed and swallowed it in one gulp.

"Ha!" Ceridwen said, returning to her proper shape. "That will teach you, little thief."

But, hidden in her stomach, Gwion Bach began to change.

A week went by, then a month, and Ceridwen's stomach started to feel very strange. It swelled up, big and round, just as if she was going to have a baby.

"Gwion Bach," she said. "You'd better come out of there, or else."

Gwion stayed exactly where he was. He curled up and slept for nine whole months and, at the end of that time, Ceridwen felt very strange indeed. She went to bed and soon she had given birth to a baby boy.

And, oh, he was so cute! His face was chubby and round, his eyes as blue as the sky and a little piece of hair curled on his forehead, the colour of golden corn.

Ceridwen's heart melted. She knew at once she couldn't hurt the baby – but she couldn't keep him either, not after he'd stolen all that magic from her. So, as the sun rose over the lake, she took a little basket and put the baby inside, then she sent the basket sailing away across the water to find a new home.

The basket floated most of that day, across the lake and along the river beyond, until, as the sun was setting, it landed at the feet of a young prince. The prince carried the baby home with great excitement, and from that day he raised the boy as his own son. He called him Taliesin, which means "shiny forehead", because princes can have strange ideas about naming babies.

Right from when Taliesin was a little boy, his head was full of knowledge. He could understand the speech of animals and birds, he sang, he composed poems, he could play any musical instrument. When he spoke, kings would stop what they were doing just to listen to him.

Taliesin the Bard grew up to be famous all over Wales. But he never forgot that before he was Taliesin, he was a tiny seed of corn, and before he was a seed, he was a crow, and before he was a crow, he was a fish, and before he was a fish, he was a hare. And before all that, he was a little boy called Gwion Bach who loved to ask questions.

The Girl from Llyn-y-Fan-Fach

Y Ferch o Llyn-y-Fan-Fach

You will see the words "llyn" and "fan" in lots of Welsh place names. Llyn is the Welsh word for "lake", and a "fan" is one of the small hills that you will find all over Wales, and especially in the Brecon Beacons, where this story takes place.

There once was a boy called Tomos who lived on a farm near a lake called Llyn-y-Fan-Fach, which means "the lake by the small hill". His job was to look after the sheep, which he enjoyed doing because it was easy. Every day he'd fill his pockets with sandwiches and he'd take the sheep to one of the fields by the lake, where he'd sit and dream until it was time to go home.

One day he was sitting as usual when he saw something very strange. There was a girl sitting on the lake. Not in the lake, or by the lake, but right on top of the blue water, her legs curled underneath her as if she was sitting on grass.

His eyes were playing tricks on him, Tomos thought. He jumped up and ran to the edge of the lake, expecting the girl to disappear, but she was still there. He took a step into the lake and his feet sank, just like feet were supposed to do in water.

"Excuse me," Tomos called.

The girl stood up and her feet didn't sink. "Yes? What do you want?"

You're standing on water, Tomos thought. Should he say something? But no, you wouldn't just stand on water accidentally without knowing it.

Now he didn't know what to say at all. He dug

in his pocket, his cheeks burning, and he found a sandwich he'd been saving for later. "Would you like a cheese sandwich?" he asked.

Would you like a cheese sandwich? He couldn't believe he'd just said that. The girl would think he had cheese for brains.

The girl laughed, and then she ran across the lake to join him. Tomos held out the sandwich again and she took it and nibbled a corner. Her nose wrinkled. "Your bread's all dry," she said. "Try again tomorrow."

With that, she ran back to the middle of the lake and vanished.

Tomos stood, staring after her. Of course she wouldn't want a smelly old sandwich that had been in his pocket all day. What had he been thinking? But she'd said to try again tomorrow. She wanted to see him again. He went home, his mind in a whirl.

The next morning, he got up early, snatched a loaf of bread out of the oven and made sandwiches while it was still hot. He wrapped them carefully, then he got the sheep together and went down to the lake.

He sat there most of the day, watching the blue water. Then, just as he was beginning to think he must have fallen asleep yesterday and dreamed the girl, he saw her again, sitting on the lake, right where she'd been before.

Tomos waved and ran to the water's edge. The girl ran to meet him and they both stood, Tomos with his feet on land and the girl with her feet on the water.

"I've brought you another sandwich," Tomos said. He held out the carefully wrapped package.

The girl opened the packet and her nose wrinkled when she saw the soggy, half-baked bread. "Your bread's far too soft," she said, sounding as if she was trying not to laugh. "You'll have to try again tomorrow."

With that, she vanished back into the lake.

When Tomos got home he asked his mother if he could bake the bread the next day. He got up extra early to put the dough in the oven and he waited until the bread was perfectly baked and cooled. Then he set off for the lake.

The girl was waiting for him, standing on the blue water near the shore, tapping one foot impatiently.

"Here," Tomos said. "Breakfast. My name's Tomos, by the way."

The girl took the loaf, broke it in half and tried some. "It's perfect," she said. "You can call me Nell."

From that day on, Nell often came out of the lake to talk to Tomos while he watched the sheep. He didn't tell anyone else about her; he didn't think they'd believe him. Then, as the years went by and Tomos's friends started getting married, he thought he ought to get married too.

"Will you marry me?" he asked Nell.

She smiled at him. "I'd love to. But you'll have to ask my father first."

Her father? She'd never mentioned anything about her family before.

The lake began to bubble in the middle. A moment later, a stern-looking man rose out of the water. Two girls stood either side of him, both of them identical to Nell.

Tomos took a few quick steps back, staring.

"So, you wish to marry my daughter?" the stern man said. "Can you prove you love her more than anyone else?"

Nell leaned towards Tomos. "Watch our feet," she whispered.

Her father clapped his hands and he and Nell and the other two girls vanished then reappeared with all three girls standing in a row.

"If you love Nell more than anyone, you'll be

able to tell her apart from her sisters," the stern man said.

This wasn't fair. They all looked exactly the same. Even their dresses were the same.

What had Nell said? Watch their feet.

Tomos looked down. He saw that two of the girls were standing straight, their feet pressed closely together. But the third girl had moved her right foot forward, as if she was about to take a step towards the shore.

Tomos waded into the lake and took her hands. "This one," he said. "This is Nell."

Nell's father frowned. "Marriages with mortals are always full of trouble. But if you both wish to marry, I will give my permission, and as a wedding gift I will give you as many cattle, horses and sheep as Nell can count in a single breath. But," he added, "if you ever strike Nell with iron, she will return to the lake and you'll never see her again."

That seemed an easy promise to make. "I won't ever strike Nell with anything," Tomos said. "I love her."

Nell drew in a huge breath and began to count. One, two, three, four, five. One-two-three-four-five. Onetwothreefourfive. Faster and faster. As she counted, a procession of pure white cows and sheep, goats and horses walked out of the lake and stopped on the shore.

Finally, Nell ran out of breath. Her father kissed her and shook hands with Tomos. "Remember your promise," he said, then he and Nell's sisters sank back into the lake and vanished.

Tomos took Nell home and they were married. They lived together happily for many years, and Nell had three baby boys.

Then, one day, when the eldest boy was about ten years old, the family decided to go out for a horse ride around the lake.

It was a beautiful sunny morning and the boys were eager to set off. But Nell wanted to make sandwiches for everyone and she hadn't even put her horse's bridle on.

Finally, she came out of the house, carrying a picnic basket. Tomos threw the bridle for her horse to her. "Hurry up," he said. "We're all waiting for you."

The bridle hit Nell on the arm.

She stopped still, her face turning pale.

The bridle bit, Tomos thought. It was made of iron.

He started forward. "No. I didn't mean it. It was an accident."

Nell shook her head, her eyes filling with tears.

She turned away from Tomos, away from her home, and she started to walk along the road to the lake.

As she walked, she counted. One, two, three, four, five. One, two, three, four, five. She counted slowly, as if she was trying to stretch this moment out for as long as she could.

As she counted, cows and sheep, goats and horses left their fields and followed her along the road to the lake.

Tomos ran after her. His sons ran behind, not understanding what was happening.

Nell reached the lake and turned back to look at her family one last time, then, sadly, she walked into the water and all the animals walked in after her, until every one of them had disappeared beneath the surface.

"Where's Mam gone?" the oldest boy asked, but Tomos could only shake his head while tears ran down his cheeks.

All summer long, Tom walked around and around the lake, hoping to catch sight of Nell, but he never did. But one day in autumn, his children ran into the house excitedly.

"We've seen Mam," they said. "She said she can't

come home and she can't see you any more, but she will visit us at the lake."

Tomos wiped the tears from his eyes. "Then I'd better bake you some bread for her," he said.

The Fairy Harp

TELYN Y TYLWYTH TEG

This is another story about the Tylwyth Teg. It also features an eisteddfod, which is a big celebration of the creative arts with competitions for all sorts of things – writing, dancing and, of course, music. In the original story, Morgan is an old man, but in this story I've made him a boy.

There was once a boy called Morgan who was good at a lot of things and he knew it. In fact, it wasn't enough for him to just be good at things: he wanted to be the best. In school, he always had to be top of the class. On sports days, he'd sulk if he came second in a race. He cheated at games until his friends refused to play with him any more.

"They're just jealous because I win all the time," Morgan would say, which wasn't true at all.

But there was one thing that Morgan was very definitely not good at: music. When he tried to sing, it sounded like a horse braying. He couldn't get the hang of any musical instrument either. He'd tried them all, hoping to find one he could be good at, but it was no use. The flute left him out of breath, the violin made his arms ache, the piano seemed to turn his fingers into clumsy sausages. He'd tried playing the drums once, and the neighbours on both sides had rushed into the street thinking their houses were about to fall down.

"Nobody's good at everything," Morgan's mother said. This was true, and maybe if Morgan had lived somewhere else he might not have minded so much. But he lived right in the middle of Wales, and Wales, as everyone knew, was the Land of Song, famous for its music. A Welshman who can't sing is like a whale who can't swim.

Morgan's friends thought it was hilarious. "Here comes Morgan the Songless," they'd laugh. "Hey, Morgan, sing us a song!" It was a bit mean, but Morgan boasted so much about being the best at everything else that they were pleased to find something he *wasn't* good at.

Every time they laughed, Morgan would grit his teeth and pretend to smile, because he had to be the best at taking a joke. Then he would go home and kick his bedroom door in rage. It wasn't fair. He could do everything else, so why couldn't he make music?

One day, the headmaster at the village school announced that the school would be holding an eisteddfod, a festival celebrating stories and music and performance, at the end of the summer term. There would be prizes for reciting poetry and for music and singing, and the very best person in the eisteddfod would win a gold crown. Or, at least, a cardboard crown painted gold with plastic jewels glued on.

The moment the head teacher talked about the crown, Morgan wanted it. He didn't care that it wasn't a proper crown. He imagined himself standing on the school stage with the crown on his head and everybody clapping because he was the best.

He was still imagining it when he left school to go home that afternoon.

His friends jostled around him. "I'm going to enter the singing prize," one of them said.

"I'll play the piano," said another. "What about you, Morgan?"

Morgan had a piano at home – his parents had bought it two Christmases ago and he'd played it for a month before giving up.

"It's a secret," Morgan said. "But I can tell you now, I'm going to win."

Everyone laughed. Morgan's face turned red with fury. "Laugh all you like," he said. "I'll show you. I'll win the music prize. I'm better than all of you."

"But, Morgan, you can't win everything," Morgan's dad said, when Morgan told him what had happened. "Why don't you enter the poetry prize and leave the music to your friends?"

But Morgan couldn't do that. He'd already told his friends he was going to win.

Straight after dinner, he went into the front room, blew the dust off the piano lid and tried to remember the notes of "Ar Hyd y Nos" – "All Through the Night". But his fingers kept slipping off the right keys and on to the wrong ones, and when they slipped he banged out the wrong note twice as loud as the rest. Morgan had only been playing for an hour when the neighbour started hammering on the wall and Morgan had to stop.

The next few weeks were musical torture. Morgan's friends sang as they walked to school. They didn't want to play rugby in the evenings because they were busy practising their instruments. And every single time they talked about the competition, it seemed to Morgan that they looked at him and laughed. Morgan began to wish he hadn't boasted quite so hard about being the best, and he really wished he hadn't said he'd win the music prize. But he couldn't take it back now. He had to keep practising.

With only a week to go until the eisteddfod, Morgan sat at his piano and plonked out the notes of "Ar Hyd y Nos" over and over again. Or, at least, he plonked out notes and some of them were in "Ar Hyd y Nos".

Morgan's dad put his head around the door. "Your

mum and I are going for a walk," he said. He had a slightly pained expression on his face. "We won't be long."

Mum and Dad were always going out for walks these days.

A little while later, the neighbour came knocking on the front door. "Can you stop playing 'Happy Birthday'? It's not even anyone's birthday."

"It's not 'Happy Birthday'," Morgan said, shutting the door. Mum and Dad didn't want to listen and his neighbour couldn't even tell what he was playing. How was he supposed to win the eisteddfod? He went back to the piano and started from the beginning, banging out each note over and over again.

He'd reached the second verse when there was a thunderous hammering at the front door.

This time, it wasn't the neighbour. Instead, a strange-looking man stood on the doorstep. He wasn't very much taller than Morgan himself, and he wore a green suit with a brown hat on his head and a brown cloak over his shoulders.

"Hello," said the man, "I've come from the Otherworld. Are you the one who's playing 'Happy Birthday' all the time?"

Morgan's face grew warm. "It's not 'Happy

Birthday', it's 'Ar Hyd y Nos' and I'm practising. My school eisteddfod is next week and I need to win the music prize."

"You mean you're going to carry on playing for a whole week?" The stranger sounded horrified. "The fairy queen's daughter is trying to sleep and you keep waking her up."

Morgan didn't believe in fairies. His friends must have got together to play a joke on him, he thought. Well, he'd play along with it. He was the best at jokes. "I'm sorry," he said, "but there's nothing I can do. I've said I'll win the music prize at the eisteddfod and that's exactly what I'm going to do."

The strange man took off his hat and scratched his head. "How about if I help you win at the eisteddfod? Will you promise to stop practising then?"

Morgan looked at the man suspiciously. There was something odd about him, now that he thought about it. Morgan was certain he'd never seen him before, even though he knew everyone in the village.

"All right," Morgan said. "Make me the best musician in the school so I can win the eisteddfod and I promise I'll never touch the piano again."

"You have a deal," said the strange man. He

whistled, clapped his hands three times and plucked a harp out of thin air. Morgan blinked. It had to be a trick, but he couldn't see how the man had done it. The harp was small enough to be tucked under one arm and it was made of plain, dark brown wood with no decorations. It didn't look very special.

"I'm supposed to win the eisteddfod on that?" Morgan asked suspiciously.

The man gave him a sharp look and ran his hand over the harp strings. Immediately, the air rang with music so beautiful that Morgan's eyes filled with tears. The sound made him think of green forests and rushing water and birds soaring high over mountains. The next moment, the man played a lively dance and Morgan's feet began to tap all by themselves.

"This is a fairy harp," the man said. "It cannot be played badly – not even by you."

"Thanks very much," Morgan said sarcastically.

The man ignored him. "Its music comes from the magic of kindness. Play with a kind heart and it will bring joy to everyone who hears. But unkindness will break it." He held the harp out to Morgan.

Morgan took it eagerly and ran his fingers across the strings. "Ar Hyd y Nos" rang out, each note perfect.

"This is *amazing*," Morgan breathed.

But when he looked up, the strange man had vanished. A cold breeze rippled down the street and made Morgan shiver. He realized now this couldn't be a joke played by his friends.

Morgan took the harp inside and hid it in his wardrobe. The next day, he listened to his friends singing as they walked to school and he smiled to himself. When they wanted to practise at lunchtime instead of playing, he shrugged. When they laughed at him, he didn't care.

That evening, he told his parents he'd decided to give up the piano and his parents said that was a coincidence because they'd decided to give up going for walks. And the neighbour gave up banging on the wall, so everyone was happy.

The day of the eisteddfod came. Morgan took his harp to school hidden in his school bag.

At the end of the day, everybody gathered in the school hall for the music contest. Morgan sat and fidgeted while, one by one, his classmates went forward to sing or play an instrument. Morgan clapped each one while secretly looking forward to the looks on their faces when they heard his harp.

Finally, the head teacher stood up. "Well," he said, "I believe that is everybody, so . . ."

"Wait!" Morgan shouted, putting his hand up. "I haven't played yet."

The whole hall burst out laughing. The head teacher bellowed for everyone to be quiet. "Are you sure you want to play?" he asked. "You don't have to."

"But I want to," Morgan said. He ran to fetch his harp.

A few people were still laughing when he returned. Morgan walked past them all to the front of the hall, took a deep breath and touched the harp strings.

The sniggering stopped. The head teacher's mouth fell open into an O of astonishment.

Morgan played "Ar Hyd y Nos", he played "Men of Harlech", he played "Cwm Rhondda". He played every tune he could think of and many more that he didn't know at all. No one made a sound. They sat, staring at him, their eyes wide, caught up in the music.

Then Morgan launched into a lively jig and the entire front row jumped up and started to dance. The second row joined in, then the third, and soon everybody was dancing. Even the head teacher slapped his knees and laughed as he leaped and twirled.

Morgan played on and on and everyone in the hall danced as if they were unable to stop. The head teacher's face turned scarlet, and people were gasping and panting for breath as their arms and legs jerked. It seemed that while the harp played, they had to dance. It was the funniest thing Morgan had ever seen.

"That'll teach you," he laughed. "I'm the best at music! I'm the best at everything!"

With that, the harp strings broke with a loud twang. A single, discordant note echoed through the hall and died away. Everybody stopped dancing and stood, scratching their heads and wondering what had happened.

Morgan looked at the broken pieces of wood and wire in his hands and he remembered what the strange man had said. *Play with a kind heart and it will bring joy to everyone who hears. But unkindness will break it.*

Morgan dropped the pieces of harp on to the floor. "I'm sorry," he said. "I'm not the best at music. I'm the worst. I cheated."

He crept out of the hall with his head down, but then he heard his friends calling his name.

"Morgan! Morgan, that was a great joke. How did you make us all dance?"

"I didn't," Morgan said. He told them about the strange man and the harp. He could tell they didn't really believe him.

"Well, it was a funny trick," they said, "and it serves us right for laughing at you. Let's go back and get our prizes."

Morgan didn't win the prize for music, but he didn't care. He put the broken pieces of harp in his bag and from that day on, instead of trying to be the best at everything, he tried to be the kindest. If unkindness had broken the harp, maybe kindness would cause it to magically mend.

The harp never did mend itself, but Morgan had lots of friends and he was always known as someone who loved a joke. As for the strange man from the Otherworld, Morgan never saw him again.

The Leaves That Hung but Never Grew

Y Dail a Hongia Heb Dyfu

I came across this story by accident: the first page was displayed as a print in a hotel where my husband was staying and, knowing how much I love folk tales, he sent me a photograph. Having read that one page, I had to hunt out the rest of the story. It's from a collection of Welsh Romani tales by John Sampson, long out of print. I love it because it is strange and magical. The girl in the original story has no name, but I've called her Seren, which means star, because she really is the star of this story.

In a lonely cottage in the Welsh mountains there lived a mother with her daughter, whose name was Seren. Seren's mother was one of those people who were full of good advice.

Always be polite and say "please" and "thank you".

Start work early in the morning so you don't waste the day.

If you're faced with something scary, do it quickly and you'll find it's not so bad after all.

Unfortunately, you can't eat advice, and Seren and her mother were so poor that they went hungry a lot of the time. When Seren's twelfth birthday came, she looked at her birthday cake, which was made of leaves, and she decided she was old enough to go out and seek her fortune.

She got up early the next morning so she wouldn't waste the day, then she put on her apron, packed a crust of bread in her handkerchief, kissed her mother goodbye and set off.

The sun was bright and she sang to herself as she walked. After a while, though, her feet began to ache, so she was very glad when she saw a house. It was a big house, surrounded by orchards and gardens with fountains. Seren saw a gardener raking up leaves on the lawn and she hurried over to him.

"Excuse me," she said, "who owns this house? I'm looking for work."

The gardener took his cap off and scratched his head. "You'll be better off looking elsewhere. The young master of the house was taken by a wicked witch and is surely dead – he was only your age, the poor boy. His uncle is the master now, and he's not the friendliest person, if you know what I mean."

He went back to raking leaves. Seren watched for a little while, wondering if she should take his advice. But her feet were aching quite a lot.

If you're faced with something scary, do it quickly, she thought. Seren made sure her apron was straight, smoothed her hands over her hair and marched up to the front doors of the house.

On her third knock, the door flew open.

A man glared down at her. He was tall and thin and he looked as if he'd come from a funeral – his clothes were black and he had a black handkerchief tucked into his black pocket.

"Who are you and what do you want?" he snapped. "My nephew is dead and I'm supposed to be in mourning."

Seren felt her knees quiver. "If you please, sir," she said, "my name is Seren and I'm looking for work.

I'm strong and I know how to cook and clean and chop wood."

"I've already got people to do all that," the man said. "If you want something to do, go and find me the leaves that hung but never grew. Good luck."

He slammed the door in Seren's face.

What a rude man, Seren thought. She'd show him – she'd find the leaves – and she wouldn't hand them over until he'd said please.

She walked on, across the fields, and soon she came to a river with trees on either side – and peeping out at her from a hazel tree was a little man. Seren could tell straight away he was one of the magical Fair Folk who lived in Wales. He was only half her height and his ears had pointed tips.

"Good afternoon," Seren said politely.

"Good afternoon," said the little man. "What's a young girl like you doing out here all by yourself?"

"I'm on a quest," Seren said. "I'm looking for the leaves that hung but never grew. Do you know where they are?"

The little man turned pale. "The leaves that hung but never grew? It is said that the very first tree to grow in these mountains had no leaves, just seven silver branches that reached to the sky. Then one night there was a terrible storm and the tree was struck by lightning. In the morning, seven golden leaves hung, one from each branch. Those leaves are full of the most powerful magic and can grant any wish you can imagine. The Fair Folk plucked them from the tree and kept them safe, but a long time ago they were stolen by a wicked witch. Go home, young miss, or you'll be eaten."

Seren laughed. "I'm not afraid of witches. If I find the leaves, what should I do with them?"

"Bury them under this tree," the little man said. "We'll take them back to the Otherworld and you will have good fortune for the rest of your life. Though, if I were you, I'd forget all this and go home."

"I think I'll carry on for a little while," Seren said. She waved goodbye and walked on.

She didn't see another person for the rest of the day. Then, as evening fell, she came to the edge of a forest, and tucked among the trees was a little house with roses growing up the walls and a curl of smoke rising from the chimney.

That's strange, Seren thought. *A house all by itself and looking so neat and tidy. Who could live here?* Maybe it was the wicked witch. But Seren had been walking most of the day by now and she'd eaten her crust of bread long ago. She had to find somewhere she could stay for the night. And so she walked up to the cottage and knocked on the door.

It was opened by an old lady wearing a flowery apron and a big smile. She didn't look anything like a wicked witch, to Seren's relief.

"Good evening," Seren said. "My name is Seren and I'm looking for work. I'm strong and I'm good at cooking and cleaning and I can chop wood."

The old lady's cheeks dimpled. "As you can see, my house is already clean and tidy, but what are you like with animals? I could use someone to look after my black boar. Why don't you come inside?"

Seren looked around the garden. She couldn't see any shed or sty where the boar might be kept. She stepped through the door, wondering, and then she stopped in amazement.

The single downstairs room was perfectly clean and tidy, except for one corner. That corner was covered in dirty straw, and on the straw lay a black boar wearing a silver collar, chained to the wall with a silver chain.

The old lady bustled about, fetching bread and cheese and cold meat as if it was the most normal thing in the world to keep a boar in your living room.

"Why do you keep the boar inside?" Seren asked.

The old lady's expression became cross for a second. "I like the company," she said. "Now, wash your hands and come and sit down. You can stay with me as long as you like. You can sleep in front of the fire where it's warm. You look after the boar and I'll look after you."

It seemed like a good deal to Seren, who was enjoying her first proper meal for as long as she could remember. She looked over at the boar, hunched miserably in the corner. What kind of person kept a boar in their house? Was the old lady a witch, or was she just a very strange old lady? She'd stay here, Seren decided, and she'd see what she could find out about the leaves that hung but never grew.

A week went by, and then another. Seren made herself busy, clearing out the old straw from the boar's corner and giving the animal fresh hay to lie on. After a few days, the old lady let her chop wood for the fire and sweep the stone floor of the cottage. The only place she wouldn't let Seren go was up the flight of stairs to the bedroom. Every night, the old lady went up the stairs alone, warning Seren to stay by the fire.

This was all very strange. Seren wondered if the

old lady might be a witch after all. Seren remembered what the little man had said – that the leaves that hung but never grew were stolen by a wicked witch. If the old lady was the witch, it would be safer to watch and wait for her chance to search for the leaves.

One night it was especially cold and the wind blew down the chimney and made Seren shiver. She took her blanket and curled up in the corner next to the boar. "Poor boar," she said. "It's not much fun to be chained up here. I wish I could help you."

"Don't feel sorry for me," the boar said. "Feel sorry for yourself. When the witch has killed and eaten me, she'll turn you into a sow and you'll be the one chained in the corner."

Seren screamed in surprise.

"Not so loud," said the boar.

"But . . . but you can talk. Why didn't you say something before?"

"I can only speak if I'm spoken to," the boar said. "You've never said a single word to me before – which is a bit rude, I might add."

Seren blushed in embarrassment. "I'm sorry. I came here looking for the leaves that hung but never grew. I heard they'd been stolen by a wicked witch. Is she . . .?" She looked up at the ceiling.

The boar nodded its great head. "She is the witch. She takes her true form at night."

Seren wondered what that true form might be and she shivered. "I'm not afraid of witches," she said, not entirely truthfully. "If you will help me find the leaves, I will help you escape."

"Finding them is easy, escaping is not so easy," said the boar. "First you must go upstairs – as quietly as you can or you'll wake the witch. Go to her bed and put your hand under her pillow. There you'll feel a leather purse. That's where she keeps the leaves. Be very careful. If you wake her, she will kill you for sure."

Seren looked at the narrow staircase, its top completely swallowed up by darkness. *If you're faced with something scary, do it quickly.* Seren got up and tiptoed to the staircase.

One step at a time, she crept up the stairs, freezing to the spot every time a floorboard squeaked. The stairs seemed to go up and up for ever, and as she climbed she heard a terrible noise of sucking and growling. Then she reached the top and realized what it was.

The witch was snoring.

Wheeeeze-growl-umph, wheeeze-growl-umph.

As Seren's eyes got used to the dark, she saw that the floor was thick with dust and strewn with rubbish and rotten food. Flies buzzed about and long strings of cobweb hung from the ceiling. The witch lay in a black bed, right in the middle of the room.

Wheeeeze-growl-umph, wheeeze-growl-umph.

Seren picked her way through the mess on the floor, her heart beating so hard she thought it would shoot right out of her chest. The witch didn't look like a nice old lady now. The hands that clutched the sheets looked like claws; the face that poked out was grey and covered in blotches and boils that wriggled every time the witch snored.

Wheeeeze-growl-umph.

Seren reached out a trembling hand and eased her fingers underneath the witch's pillow.

Wheeeeze-growl-umph, wheeeze-Growl-UMPH.

The tip of Seren's finger touched something leathery.

The purse, Seren thought. She tugged it gently out and fled back across the room.

Wheeeeze-growl-umph.

The witch's snoring settled back to its previous horrid volume.

Seren scraped cobwebs off her face, feeling sick

and dizzy. She crept back down the stairs as quickly as she dared.

"Do you have it?" the boar asked.

Seren nodded. She opened the purse and saw seven golden leaves, each one looking as fresh as if they'd only just been picked. She put her hand in the purse. "I wish the boar was free and I wish we both escape from here."

The silver collar around the boar's neck snapped. The boar reared up on to its back legs, and then it wasn't a boar at all, but a boy, about Seren's own age.

Seren gasped in amazement. "I visited a house in the middle of orchards and fountains where the young master had been taken by a witch. Is that you?"

"It is," the boy said. "My uncle came to look after me when my parents died, but he's cruel and horrible. I started going on long walks to get away from him, but I walked too far from home and the witch caught me. I bet my uncle is pretending to be sad I'm gone."

"We'll worry about your uncle later," Seren said firmly. "First, we need to escape."

At that moment, they heard the witch's voice. "Seren? Is that you? What are you doing?"

They both froze in fright. But the poker jiggled

in the fireplace. “I’m just putting more wood on the fire,” it called in Seren’s voice.

“Quickly,” Seren whispered. She took the boy’s hand and they ran to the door.

Upstairs, the bed creaked and the witch shouted again. “Seren, where are you? Come upstairs.”

The broom jiggled in the corner. “I’m on my way!”

Seren opened the door.

“Seren!” bellowed the witch. “Where is my purse? Where are the leaves that hung but never grew?”

This time there was no answer. Seren and the boy were running for their lives.

The witch ran downstairs. She saw the empty room, the broken collar lying on the floor and the door swinging open. She grabbed the broom and jumped on. “Follow them,” she commanded.

She had enough magic of her own to command objects in her own home. The broom rose into the air.

Seren and the boy heard the witch roaring behind them. Seren opened the purse and put her hand on the leaves. “I wish that we were hidden from the witch,” she panted.

Straight away, she turned into a duck and the boy turned into a stream of water.

The witch landed her broomstick in the grass a moment later. "Duck!" she shouted. "Have you seen a girl and a boy running this way?"

The duck quacked and dived under the water.

The witch shouted in rage and flew on. Soon, the broom began to tremble. "Fly faster," the witch commanded, kicking it. But she no longer had the magic leaves and her own power was fading. The broom suddenly stopped and then crashed to the ground, and the witch fell on her head and died.

The duck and the stream heard the thud as the witch landed, and they turned back into Seren and the boy.

"Come on," Seren said, and they ran again. As morning broke through the clouds, they arrived at the boy's house. His uncle threw open the door and nearly fell over in surprise when he saw them.

"Seren saved me," the boy said. "I want her to come and live here with us."

Seren could see from the uncle's face what he thought of that idea. The look in his eyes was as hard as stone. "No," he said. "I asked her to find the leaves that hung but never grew and she brought you back instead. She can go away right this minute."

"Oh, I have the leaves," Seren said. She took the

purse out of her pocket and showed it to him. The boy's uncle tried to grab it but Seren put it back in her pocket. "I'll give them to you later," she said, thinking that as soon as he had the leaves he'd throw her out of the house. "But first, we are both very tired and we'd like to rest."

The boy's uncle twisted his mouth into a smile, though his eyes flashed with anger. "I suppose you'd better come in. I'll have a bedroom prepared for you."

Seren and the boy sat in the kitchen and ate breakfast together, then the uncle escorted Seren to a room and showed her a huge four-poster bed with a heavy canopy over it.

"Here you are," he said, sounding friendly all of a sudden. "Sleep well."

Seren lay down but she couldn't get comfortable. The bed was soft and she was too used to sleeping on the witch's stone floor. She got up off the bed and lay down on the carpet, and soon she was asleep. She may have even snored a little.

Suddenly Seren was woken by a great crash. She jumped up, her heart thumping wildly, and she saw that the canopy had fallen down on the bed, crushing the mattress underneath.

People came running into her room at the noise. The boy's uncle came in last, and Seren noticed that while all the servants were pale with shock, he looked angry to see Seren standing there.

Seren put her hand in her pocket and touched the leaves. "I wish you to tell the truth," she said. "Did you try to kill me?"

The uncle turned red, then he turned white. His mouth twisted into twenty different shapes as he struggled not to speak. "Yes!" he finally burst out. "I want the leaves and I don't want a poor girl like you being friends with my nephew. I'll keep trying to kill you until I succeed."

Everybody was horrified. The servants called for the guards and the uncle was taken off to prison.

The boy didn't seem very upset about his uncle. He was more worried that Seren might have been hurt. He sent a servant to fetch Seren's mother so they could all live together in the grand house.

While they were waiting, Seren took the purse of leaves and walked across the fields to the river. There, she buried them under the hazel tree where the fairy man had told her.

When she returned to the mansion, she found that her mother had arrived. From that day on, she and her mother and the boy lived together very happily and they enjoyed good fortune for the rest of their lives.

The Devil and Giant Jack

Y Diafol a Jac y Cawr

Near the Welsh market town of Abergavenny, you will find Skirrid Fawr – Big Skirrid. Its Welsh name is Ysgryd, which means "split", and if you see it, you will know why. A large part of the mountain peak is missing, making it look as though the peak is split in two. The missing bit of mountain stands nearby in a separate hill which is called Skirrid Fach – Little Skirrid.

Geologists will tell you this came about because of a landslide, but that's because geologists don't know about the devil and Giant Jack. Here's a set of three stories. The first two are different versions of how Mount Skirrid got its name. I've included them both so you can decide which one is most believable. The third story comes from the end of Giant Jack's life and shows just how clever he was.

1.

If you climb to the top of Mount Skirrid, you'll see a large, flat stone on the summit, looking a bit like a table. This stone is called the Devil's Table because, as everybody knows, the devil used to come here to play cards with Giant Jack.

Now, the devil in Welsh stories is very different to the devil you may hear about elsewhere. He loves playing tricks on people but he's not half as clever as he thinks he is, and so, in Wales at least, he is always being outwitted. You'll often see him stamping about the Black Mountains in a bad mood because of this.

Giant Jack had known the devil for a long time and he wasn't afraid of him in the slightest. Jack's real name was Jack O'Kent and he lived in the border country between England and Wales. He was a magician and people called him Giant Jack because . . . well, if you want to invite Jack round for dinner, you'd better make it a picnic in the garden, otherwise Jack might accidentally pull your front door off its hinges and break all your furniture. Or put his head through your ceiling.

One warm day, Jack and the devil were sitting on the gently rounded peak of Mount Skirrid. It wasn't called Mount Skirrid then, of course. Between the devil and the giant lay the large, flat rock called the Devil's Table, and on the table was a pack of cards. Some of the cards had been torn in two.

"You cheated!" the devil shouted, tearing up another card.

"You started it," Giant Jack said. "You've been cheating all day, and I've still won every game."

"Argh!" The devil hit all the cards off the table. Several of them burst into flame.

"Let's play something else," Giant Jack said, partly to keep the peace and partly because the devil had destroyed almost the entire pack of cards.

The devil folded his arms and stuck his chin on his chest in a sulk. Giant Jack grinned and stretched out his long legs, putting his boots up on the table. "Well," he said, "today is a beautiful day."

If the devil hadn't been in such a disagreeable mood, he might well have agreed. It was a day of blue sky, fluffy clouds and bright sunshine. From where they were sitting, Jack and the devil could see all the way across the fields below to the green peak of the Sugarloaf Mountain opposite. It was a good five or six miles to walk but it looked almost close enough to touch.

Jack gazed at the Sugarloaf thoughtfully. "I bet I could jump over there."

"I bet you couldn't," the devil shot back.

Giant Jack looked at the devil and raised an eyebrow. "Is this a real bet or one of your silly dares?"

The devil spluttered indignantly. "I do not make silly dares." He jumped to his feet. "I bet you ten pounds that you can't jump from here to the top of the Sugarloaf."

Giant Jack swung his huge feet off the Devil's Table and stood up. "You're on," he said. "Stand back."

He bent his knees and swung his arms. The devil scuttled back out of the way. Giant Jack drew in a breath of air so deep that all the clouds in the sky were sucked towards him. Then he let his breath out in an almighty roar, swung his arms back, and he kicked off from the mountain summit with all his strength.

For a few seconds he felt as if he was flying. He

could see the tiny shapes of people on the ground, pointing up at him. A startled bird flew past him. The Sugarloaf suddenly seemed a very long way away. Jack windmilled his arms and legs, turned a somersault, rolled up in a ball and tumbled.

He struck the ground with a crash that made the earth tremble. He lay, dazed, for a moment, then jumped to his feet. He was standing right on the top of the Sugarloaf. He'd done it!

"Hey, devil," he shouted, doing a victory dance on the summit. "You owe me ten pounds!"

But then he noticed there was something strange about the mountain he'd just left. The top had been a smooth and gentle curve, but now it stuck up in two jagged peaks.

There was a pop of air and the smell of sulphur. "You've broken the mountain," the devil said, appearing next to the giant.

It was true. When Jack had made his enormous leap, he'd kicked the ground so hard that he'd knocked a piece right out of the top and the rounded peak of the mountain was now split in two.

And that is how Mount Skirrid got its name.

Or maybe it isn't . . .

2.

One warm day, Jack and the devil were sitting on the gently rounded peak of Mount Skirrid. It wasn't called Mount Skirrid then, of course. Between the devil and the giant lay the large, flat rock called the Devil's Table, and on the table was a pack of cards. Some of the cards had been torn in two.

"You cheated!" the devil shouted, tearing up another card.

"You started it," Giant Jack said.

"Argh!" The devil hit all the cards off the table. Several of them burst into flame.

Giant Jack grinned and stretched out his long legs, putting his boots up on the table. "Well," he said, "today is a beautiful day."

If the devil hadn't been in such a disagreeable mood, he might well have agreed. It was a day of blue sky, fluffy clouds and bright sunshine. From where they were sitting, Jack and the devil could see all the way across the fields to the green peak of the Sugarloaf Mountain, and in the other direction, they could see the Malvern Hills in England.

"I bet I can guess what you're thinking," the devil said.

"I bet you can't," said Giant Jack. "I was thinking you're a rotten loser who cheats at cards."

The devil's face, which was already red, turned a shade redder. "Well, I bet you can't guess what *I'm* thinking."

"Go on, then," Jack said. "What are you thinking?"

The devil didn't want to admit he'd merely been admiring the scenery. He turned from side to side, slowly. "I was wondering," he said, puffing his chest out a little, "which of those hills is taller? The ones in England or that one over by there?"

Giant Jack laughed. "I'd have thought it was obvious. It's the Sugarloaf, of course. It's much taller."

The devil hadn't cared which hill was taller until Jack spoke. Now he folded his arms stubbornly. "That shows what you know," he said. "The Malverns are taller than the Sugarloaf. Any fool can see that."

Jack scratched his head. "That's easily settled.

Let's measure them and find out. I bet you ten pounds that the Sugarloaf is taller."

"Done!" said the devil. He took off his hat and he put on a big canvas apron, full of pockets. In each pocket he had a tape measure. He clapped his hands and he and Giant Jack rose into the air and flew all the way across the countryside until they landed at the foot of the Malverns.

They measured every hill, both of them writing down the numbers in case either of them cheated. When they'd finished, the devil clapped his hands again and they flew back and landed on the slope of the Sugarloaf.

The devil unrolled the first tape measure, then the second, then the third, and on and on.

Giant Jack began to chuckle. "The Sugarloaf is taller."

"No, it's not," the devil snapped. "Be quiet and help me measure."

When they'd finished, the devil flew them back to the Devil's Table, where they'd made the bet. "So the highest hill in the Malverns is four hundred and twenty five metres . . .." said the devil, turning the pages of his notebook. "And the Sugarloaf is . . ." His face turned scarlet.

"Five hundred and ninety-six metres," said Giant Jack, snatching the notebook from the devil's hand. "You lost!"

The devil stamped his foot. "I'll show you!" He shook out his apron and scooped up a giant heap of earth from the top of the mountain, then he took off into the sky. "I'll put this on the Malverns," he shouted, "then we'll see which mountain is bigger."

But the apron of earth was so heavy that the devil could barely fly, and soon he heard the sound of tearing and he saw the heavy canvas of his apron begin to rip.

"No!" the devil yelled as his apron gave way. All the earth fell out and landed in a hill below him.

Looking back, the devil saw the jagged shape of the mountain he'd ruined, and Giant Jack standing and laughing at him.

That is how Mount Skirrid got its name. And the hill that the devil accidentally created is called Little Skirrid.

But the devil was properly angry. "I'll have the last laugh, Jack O'Kent," he shouted. "When you are dead and buried, whether it be inside the church or outside, I will come and carry you away, body and soul."

There's another story about that . . .

3.

The devil didn't visit Giant Jack very much after his humiliating defeat on Mount Skirrid. He was a very sore loser, after all. But Jack never forgot the devil's parting words. "When you are dead and buried, whether it be inside the church or outside, I will come and carry you away, body and soul."

Many years passed and Jack knew that he was getting old and he would die soon. He called all his family to his house and he made a very strange request.

"You know Grosmont Church?" he said.

Jack's relatives nodded. The church was the biggest one in Abergavenny and it had the highest, thickest walls of any church.

"Well," said Jack, "I want you to promise that when I die you'll open up one of the church walls and bury me inside it. I want to be neither inside the church nor outside it."

Jack's family were greatly puzzled by the request, but Jack had had a strange life and they knew that he wouldn't ask for something like this unless there was a very good reason.

A month later, Jack died. His family made all the arrangements and the coffin bearers came – fifty of them, because, as you'll remember, Jack was a giant – and they carried his coffin all the way to Grosmont Church.

At the church, the mourners were joined by a strange-looking man in a black suit and a top hat that smelled faintly of smoke. He sat down on the back pew of the church and he grinned all the way through the funeral service despite the vicar shooting him very cross looks.

The people finished singing the final hymn. "And now," the vicar said, "it is time to say our final farewell."

The man in the back pew giggled.

The coffin bearers came forward and picked up Jack's coffin. Then, instead of carrying it out of the church to the cemetery, they carried it across the aisle and laid in inside a hole in the church wall.

The man at the back of the church jumped up

with a shout of rage. "I don't believe it!" he yelled. "Jack O'Kent has beaten me again."

All the mourners in the church turned around to stare, but the strange man vanished, leaving behind nothing but a strong smell of smoke.

Rhiannon and her Baby

RHIANNON A'I BABI

This is the second story about Pwyll Prince of Dyfed from the Mabinogion, although this one is main about his wife, Rhiannon, and their baby son. You'll remember that Rhiannon was supposed to marry a man called Lord Gwawl, but she tricked him into letting her marry Pwyll instead.

Princess Rhiannon of Dyfed was very happy. She was married to Prince Pwyll and she loved living in his castle in Wales. Then, after they'd been married for four years something very exciting happened. Rhiannon had a baby: a boy.

Most people were very happy to hear the news, but some people started whispering together.

"Princess Rhiannon can perform magic," they said. "What if the baby is part magic? You can't trust magic."

"I always thought it was odd of Prince Pwyll to ride off and get married without tell anyone," someone else said. "I wonder if Rhiannon enchanted him into doing it."

Prince Pwyll was too excited about the new baby to pay any attention to the whispers. He chose six women from the castle and gave them the job of taking care of the tiny prince.

The six ladies, however, were more interested in the castle gossip than in looking after babies. Night after night, they sat up late, talking.

"Did you know," said one, "Princess Rhiannon was supposed to marry somebody else?"

"And did you know," the second lady said, "she rode to Dyfed all by herself, and she proposed to

Pwyll. That isn't how a princess behaves."

"It's not normal," agreed the third lady. "And everyone knows she can do magic. It's not right. Pwyll should have married a proper Welsh princess, not one from the Otherworld."

So they talked long into the night, until, one by one they all fell asleep.

In his cradle, the baby prince slept on too. No one noticed the shadow that stole across the wall, the hand that reached through the window.

But in the morning, when the ladies woke, the cradle was empty.

They all sat up in alarm.

"What are we going to do?" the first one asked. "If Pwyll finds out his child is missing, he'll banish us from the castle."

"That's if he doesn't execute us," the second lady said.

Then the third lady said something that made all the others gasp.

"We can't do that," the fourth lady said. "It's not right."

"But we must do something," the fifth lady said. "If we tell Pwyll the truth he might kill us."

The sixth lady got up and looked in the empty

cradle. "I wouldn't be surprised," she said, "if Princess Rhiannon *was* to blame for this. She comes from the Otherworld, remember People like her might do anything."

And so all six ladies started crying and wailing and they rushed to the great hall where Pwyll and Rhiannon were having breakfast.

"Terrible news!" they cried. "Princess Rhiannon has eaten her baby!"

Pwyll leaped to his feet. Rhiannon turned white. Of course she hadn't eaten her baby! Why would anyone think that?

She rushed into the baby's room and stopped when she saw the empty cradle.

"Someone's taken him," she said and she broke down crying.

Rumours raced through the palace. The baby was gone, vanished as if by magic, and the only person who could do magic was Rhiannon.

"This is what you get for marrying a magic princess," Pwyll's friends said. "If you want our advice, you'll have Rhiannon executed and marry a proper Welsh princess."

"It's a shame you can't turn her into a horse," another of the knights said. "Seeing as she likes riding horses so much."

Rhiannon couldn't believe what she was hearing, and neither could Pwyll by the look of him. But it seemed that the whole palace was turning against them.

Pwyll turned to Rhiannon with a pleading look in his eyes. She sighed. She knew what was coming – he always was too eager to please his friends.

"I've decided your punishment," Pwyll said. "For seven years, you must sit at the city gates, and when any visitors come in, you must carry them on your back through the streets, just as if you are a horse."

At least he wasn't going to execute her. Rhiannon bowed her head and nodded.

For the next six months, Rhiannon carried visitors on her back, but every time she carried someone, she also told them how her baby had vanished. Surely, she thought, someone must know what had happened to him.

The story of the lost prince spread throughout Wales, all the way to the Kingdom of Gwent where a lord called Tiernyon was hiding in a stable, watching as his favourite horse gave birth to a foal.

She was the most beautiful horse Tiernyon had

ever owned. But every time she had a foal, the foal vanished. This time, Tiernyon was determined to catch the thief.

The new foal stumbled to its feet just as the clock struck midnight. Tiernyon saw a shadow crawl across the wall. He jumped up and drew his sword, and in the same moment, a monstrous arm reached into the stable and snatched the foal from its mother's side.

Tiernyon yelled and slashed the arm with his sword. The monster dropped the foal with a shriek and fled. Tiernyon ran out of the stable after it, but it had already vanished. Instead, he saw a golden-haired child lying in the mud.

Tiernyon took the baby back to his house and woke his wife.

"This is very strange," she said. "I heard a story just the other day. Princess Rhiannon's baby disappeared some months ago. People are saying she ate the boy, but she said he vanished from his cradle in the night. I wonder if this is the same baby."

As soon as it was light, Tiernyon and his wife set off for Dyfed.

Rhiannon was sitting at the gates, dirty and tired from carrying people, but when she saw the baby she gave a great cry and swept him up in her arms, and it felt as if all the weight had been lifted from her.

Tiernyon told her what had happened and they hurried together to the castle to tell Pwyll.

"... And so," Rhiannon said, "the ladies-in-waiting and your friends were all mistaken." She turned around and looked at all the worried faces in the castle hall. She could ask Pwyll to punish everyone who'd lied about her, but then Pwyll would have to punish some of his own friends. "There's been enough punishment already," she said. "I'm just happy that we've got our baby back."

All of Pwyll's friends, especially the ones who'd suggested having her executed, turned red and shuffled their feet in shame. The six ladies-in-waiting packed up their things that day and quietly left the palace. Rhiannon didn't mind. She was just happy to have her baby back. "My worry is over," she said, and she renamed the baby Pryderi, which means 'worry' in Welsh.

Tiernyon and his wife became great friends and Prince Pryderi often went to visit them. When he grew up he became one of the greatest heroes of Wales. You can read another story about Pryderi later in this book.

Tappers in the Copper Mine

PWCA YN Y PWLL COPR

For thousands of years, Wales has had mines. Before coal, there was lead and gold and copper. And, as long as there have been mines, miners have told tales of the magical folk who live underground.

Alys didn't like the mine. She never had, even though everyone she knew worked there, digging copper out of the hard ground. The tunnels were cold and dark and so narrow you had to squeeze through sideways in places. The last time she'd ventured in, she'd started to panic, thinking she couldn't breathe.

"But the mine is safe," her older brother, Gethin, said. "The Pwca look after us."

Alys said nothing. She was fairly sure the Pwca weren't real – the fairy folk who lived in the mine and knocked on the walls to warn people of danger or show them where the best copper was. But if they *were* real, they ought to have something better to do than hang about underground and spy on ordinary people.

The one good thing was that, at ten years old, Alys was too young to work in the mine. But she knew that in a few years' time she'd have to do it. Gethin was thirteen and he went into the tunnels almost every day now. Alys's only hope was that the mine would run out of copper and her parents would have to find some other work to do.

One evening, Alys saw Gethin loading bread and cakes into a basket.

“It’s for the Pwca,” he said. “It’s our family’s turn to take food for their supper.”

Alys rolled her eyes. This was such a silly custom. Every day, someone in the town had to take a basket of food for the Pwca.

“The Pwca don’t really eat the food,” Alys said. “The rats do.”

Gethin sighed and carried on packing cakes into the basket.

Then Alys had an idea. “Can I take it?” she asked.

“You?” Gethin stared at her in surprise. “But you’re afraid to go into the mine.”

“I won’t need to go in far,” Alys said, feeling a bit breathless at her own daring. “I’m going to be starting work there in a year or two. I need to get used to it, don’t I?”

She knew Gethin was tired after working in the mine all day. She snatched the basket from the table. “I won’t be long,” she said, and she ran out before Gethin could say another word.

Once outside, Alys slowed. She walked in the direction of the mine, but she didn’t go in. She wasn’t going to take one step inside those nasty tunnels. She stopped just outside and she emptied the whole basket of food into the long grass at the side of the path.

There! she thought, watching the cakes rolls down the slope.

Now she could prove the Pwca didn't exist. Tomorrow, when everyone dug up just as much copper as usual, she'd tell Gethin what she'd done and he'd have to admit she was right.

The next day, everyone went out to work as usual. Alys waited at home, barely containing her giggles.

Gethin and Dad came home early that evening, both of them looking tired and dirty.

"We couldn't find any copper," Dad said. "Nobody could. We worked all day and we didn't bring out a single nugget."

Alys jumped with guilt. They had to be joking, but she could see from their faces that they were serious. Usually the family would sit up after supper, laughing and playing games, but tonight they all went to bed early.

Alys lay in the dark and worried. It wasn't her fault that they hadn't found any copper today. It couldn't be. The Pwca weren't real. It was just bad luck, she thought. Tomorrow, the miners would find another seam of copper and everything would be back to normal.

But the next evening, the miners came home

empty-handed again. It was as if all the copper had suddenly vanished from the hills.

"This is my fault," Gethin said. "There must have been something wrong with the food I left for the Pwca. You did put it right inside the mine entrance, didn't you, Alys?"

Alys nodded, too afraid to tell the truth. She could barely bring herself to eat. All her life, she'd hoped the mine would run out of copper so she wouldn't have to go to work there, but now she could see the fear in her parents' eyes. They made a good living from the copper, she thought – and not just Mam and Dad but everyone in the town. If the mine ran out of copper, what would people do?

She thought she'd never sleep that night, but she must have fallen asleep at some point because she woke suddenly. Looking over at Gethin's bed, she saw that it was empty.

Alys scrambled up and ran down to the kitchen. Gethin wasn't there. A scrap of paper lay on the table under a mug.

Gone to find the Pwca.

Alys sank down on to a chair, feeling hot and cold all over. She'd done this and Gethin thought it was his fault. She thought of the dark mine tunnels, even darker by night, and her hands trembled. She clenched her fists and stood up. Still feeling a little shaky, she packed a loaf of bread and one of Mam's fruit cakes into a basket and ran out of the house.

The moon was full, filling the valley with silver light. There was no sign of Gethin at all. Alys ran along the path to the mine. The wind rustled in the branches and the long grass where she'd thrown the Pwca's food.

"I'm sorry," Alys whispered.

The only reply was an owl hooting in the distance.

Alys reached the mine and stopped outside the main tunnel. "Gethin?" she called. "Gethin, are you there?"

The tunnel carried her voice back to her in echoes. *Gethin? Gethin?*

Alys waited a moment longer, then she lit a candle and stepped into the tunnel.

Straight away the air felt colder and Alys found it hard to breathe. "Hello?" she called. The candle wavered in her hand. "Gethin?" She paused. "Pwca, can you hear me? I'm sorry. I'm the one who threw away your food. I've brought some more. If you can hear me, please help me find my brother."

She hadn't really expected the Pwca to answer,

and they didn't. If she wanted to find Gethin, she'd have to do it herself. She was so stiff with fright she could barely make her legs move, but she managed to take one step, and then another. The next step was a little easier. Alys crouched down to go through a low section of tunnel. She'd never been this far into the mine before. She could hardly believe she was doing it.

Then her candle went out.

Alys stood rigid in the thick darkness, clutching her basket in one hand, the useless candle in the other, her back pressed to the cold rock. It felt like the tunnel was closing in around her, threatening to crush her. She gulped in air.

And then, through the sound of her own panicked breathing, she heard a faint tapping coming from further along the tunnel.

"Gethin?" Alys called.

Tap . . . scratch . . . tap . . . scratch.

Somehow, Alys found she could move her arms and legs. She tucked the candle into her pocket and felt her way along the tunnel, holding on to the wall.

The tapping seemed to be coming from a side tunnel now. Alys paused to listen and started along it. Her feet splashed through a puddle and she heard a rat squeak. She paused, forced herself to take a few shaky breaths, and she walked on.

Tap . . . tap . . . tap.

Another tunnel, the ceiling a little higher here. Were the Pwca really there, or was it her imagination?

And then, so faint that she thought it really was her imagination, she saw a glimmer of candlelight.

"Gethin!" she shouted.

After a moment, a cry came back. "Alys?"

Alys forgot to be afraid. She dropped her basket and she ran in the direction of the light.

The tunnel opened up suddenly into a cavern and, right the middle, Gethin was sitting on the ground.

"I tripped and twisted my ankle," he said. "I didn't think anyone would find me."

Alys ran to him. "The Pwca led me to you." She smiled in the darkness. The tunnels felt friendly to her now, almost as if they were inviting her through. She lit her candle from Gethin's and helped him to his feet. "Let's go home."

A sudden, loud tapping came from overhead. They both looked up and saw a glittering seam in the rock. "Copper!" they said together.

Was it her imagination, or had the Pwca led her to her brother and the copper? By the next morning,

Alys was no longer sure. But whenever she went into the mine after that, she always whispered a thank you and left a loaf of bread or a cake, just in case.

The Drowned Land

Y Wlad o Dan Dŵr

If you visit Cardigan Bay today, you'll see the beautiful blue waters of the Irish Sea. But once upon a time, people say, all that sea was green land.

This is one of the many stories that tells of what happened.

Long, long ago, in the north-east of Wales, there was a land called Cantre'r Gwaelod. Its name means "the land at the bottom" and it was indeed the lowest area of land in the whole of Wales. It was a beautiful place, and because it was so flat and sheltered, it was the best land in Wales for growing crops. The people of Cantre'r Gwaelod grew wheat and barley and tended orchards full of apples and plums and pears. They sold their crops all over Wales and grew rich on the profits. None of them worried that the sea was so close and so vast. The sea had never bothered the land in the past, they said, so why should it start now?

And, besides, they had the wall.

The wall stood like a giant between the land and the sea. It stretched from Bardsey Island all the way south to Cardigan town. It was ten metres high at its tallest point, and two metres thick. Halfway along it, there was a pair of gates that were opened at low tide so the fishing boats could go through, but when those gates were shut, nothing – not one single drop of seawater – could pass.

Just to make sure, the kingdom had a wallmaster. He was the second most important person in the kingdom after the king himself. It was the wallmaster's job to open and close the massive sea gates at the right time each day. And it was the wall-master's job to ride around the wall and check that every stone was holding firm. And, should the sea ever come over the wall, it was the wallmaster's job to run to the alarm tower and ring the bells to warn everybody to flee. But no wallmaster had ever had to do that, and none ever would. The wall, and the land behind it, were safe.

The wallmaster at this time was a man called Seithennyn. He'd got the job because he was friends with the king, which is probably not the best reason to give someone a job, as Seithennyn proved. He liked it when people bowed to him and called him wallmaster, and he liked the gold he was paid every month. But he was far less fond of riding the length of the wall looking for non-existent leaks, and as for the sea gates, he wished they'd never been invented. Opening and closing them every day was a heavy, tiring nuisance.

Very soon, Seithennyn started leaving the daily wall inspections to his apprentice, Gwilym. He'd have let Gwilym take care of the sea gates too, but the boy was only just fourteen and too small to turn the wheel that opened and closed them, so

Seithennyn had to do it himself. He grumbled about it every day.

Gwilym didn't care about his master's grumbling. He was proud to be the wallmaster's apprentice. It was up to him to keep everyone safe and he took his duty seriously. More than once, he called Seithennyn out to look at a crack in the wall, only to find the crack was a bit of seaweed, or a mark on one of the stones.

"Still, it's better to be safe than sorry," Gwilym said.

"We're already safe," Seithennyn sneered. "The wall has stood for a hundred years and the sea has never come in. What makes you think it'll come in now?"

Gwilym reddened. He knew it was silly to worry, but he couldn't forget about the sea that thundered on the other side of the wall. He couldn't forget the fact that it only needed one hole in the wall, one mistake, for all that water to come pouring in.

But the sea did not come pouring in. The winter storms came and went and the wall held fast. As the days grew warmer, Gwilym allowed himself to relax a little. Seithennyn was right: the wall had stood for a century and it wasn't suddenly going to fall apart for no reason.

Spring came and the king announced a banquet at the palace to celebrate. Hundreds of people were invited, including Seithennyn, of course. Gwilym, of course, was not.

"I don't know what you're sulking about," Seithennyn said. "You didn't expect the king to invite an apprentice to the banquet, did you?"

Gwilym hadn't been sulking. He didn't like parties and he was quite happy to have a free evening at home without Seithennyn bothering him. But Seithennyn seemed to be in a bad mood today and wanted to pick on him for something. "What about the sea gates?" Gwilym asked. "Who's going to close them if you're at the palace?"

From the sudden frozen look on Seithennyn's face, Gwilym guessed his master had forgotten about the gates. "I'll close them before I go to the palace, of course," he snapped. "Now go away and stop bothering me."

Gwilym was glad to get out of his way.

That evening, a cold wind blew in off the sea. Gwilym felt it and shivered. Had Seithennyn remembered to close the sea gates? But of course Seithennyn would have remembered. He wouldn't forget something as important as that.

“Better safe than sorry,” Gwilym murmured to himself. He saddled up his horse and set off in the direction of the wall.

As he drew near, he heard a strange sound. He wasn’t sure what it was at first, as he’d never heard anything like it before. Then it hit him and his heart almost stopped in his chest.

Water. That’s what it was. The sound of water: running, flowing, pouring.

Gwilym urged his horse into a gallop. As soon as he saw the sea gates, he guessed what must have happened. Seithennyn, in his hurry to join the king’s banquet, hadn’t closed them properly. It wouldn’t have mattered at low tide when there was a strip of sand outside between the sea and the wall. But now the tide was at its highest and the pounding waves were pushing the gates further and further apart.

Gwilym jumped off his horse and raced to the wheel that operated the gates. He heaved until black spots danced in front of his eyes, but it was no use. He couldn’t even manage to turn the wheel at low tide and now, with the sea forcing its way through, it was impossible.

Gwilym jumped back on to his horse. He had to warn people. He rode as fast as he could back to town. People turned to stare as he slid off the horse and ran up the steps of the alarm tower, two at a time. Gwilym hauled on the rope.

The bell, which had never been used before, moved sluggishly, and then it swung wildly.

Clang. Clang. Clang.

"The sea is coming!" Gwilym shouted. "Everyone run! The sea is coming!"

Some people laughed at him. Others screamed and fled in panic. Gwilym ran down from the tower and pushed through the crowd. He had to find Seithennyn. The palace!

He rode through the streets to the palace gates. A pair of guards barred his path.

"Where's Seithennyn?" Gwilym gasped. "The sea is coming!"

The guards stared at him in disbelief and laughed.

"You're Seithennyn's apprentice, aren't you?" one of them said. "Your master's at the party with everyone else. Go on in if you want, but don't blame us if he boxes your ears for it."

Gwilym squeezed between them and ran inside.

The noise hit him as if he'd run into a wall. The hall was full of people, eating and drinking, laughing and talking. Musicians played in one corner, and servants weaved their way through the crowd, carrying trays. No one took the slightest notice of Gwilym as he stood, his chest heaving.

Gwilym caught hold of a servant girl.

"The sea is coming!" he shouted.

The girl started to laugh, but then she seemed to understand that he wasn't joking and her eyes widened. She dropped her tray and pushed through the hall, shaking people.

Then Gwilym saw Seithennyn slumped over a table, his head on his folded arms. Gwilym rushed to him and shook him.

"Whassatgerrof," Seithennyn mumbled, shoving him away.

"The sea is coming!" Gwilym shouted in desperation. Seithennyn pushed him away again and put his head back on his arms.

Gwilym felt someone tugging his shirt. It was the servant girl. "We warned them!" she yelled. "We have to run!"

Some of the people in the hall did seem to realize something was wrong and they were getting up, stumbling to the door. The musicians stopped playing and, without the sound of their instruments, Gwilym could hear a distant roar, growing louder.

He cast one last look back at the king's hall and then he let the girl drag him through the doors into the courtyard.

The guards had already fled, leaving Gwilym's horse standing inside the palace gates. The street outside the palace was full of people running. In the distance, Gwilym saw a dark line, topped with foamy white.

He climbed on to his horse and offered his hand to the servant girl. She climbed up behind him and they rode. Through the streets, away from the palace, away from the tumbling wall of water. They didn't stop until they reached the hills overlooking Cantre'r Gwaelod.

Gwilym slid off the horse and collapsed in the grass. The girl sat down next to him. In silence, they watched as the sea rolled across the green land, covering it completely.

To this day, people say, at low tide, you can see trees poking up from the seabed of Cardigan Bay. And, sometimes, when the wind is blowing off the sea, you might be able to hear the warning bell clanging back and forth, pushed this way and that by the waves.

The Three Calves

Y Tri Llo

You'll find many fairy tales in which three brothers compete for a prize and the youngest brother wins. Many of them involve strange journeys and magical items. This Welsh version, however, is rooted firmly in everyday life and most of the story takes place on a farm. I like it because it has a happy ending and it shows someone winning by cleverness. I feel sorry for the calves, though.

There were once two farmers who lived in the same valley in Wales. The first farmer had three sons called Tom, Dai and Sion, while the second farmer had a single daughter. Her name was Gwenllian, and she was about the same age as Sion. The two of them wanted to get married, but they hadn't told anyone yet. Sion was the youngest of the three brothers and, although he did most of the work on their family's farm, he didn't get paid anything, so saving for a wedding would be hard. Instead, Sion and Gwenllian met in secret whenever they could.

This went on for some months until, one day, Tom saw Sion sneaking away from the farm.

Where's he off to? Tom thought, and followed.

Tom liked to think he was cleverer than anyone else, so you can imagine his fury when he saw Gwenllian waiting for Sion and realized they'd been seeing each other for months without anyone noticing. He hid behind a hedge and listened to them sighing and complaining because they couldn't afford to get married.

So Sion wants to marry Gwenllian, Tom thought. *Two can play at that game.*

He rushed home and burst into the kitchen,

where his parents and Dai were sitting. "I've made a decision," he said. "I want to marry Gwenllian."

Dai scowled to hear the news. Dai was lazy – too lazy even to think for himself most of the time, so he usually copied whatever Tom did.

"No," he said, "I want to marry Gwenllian. I've been in love with her for months."

"Well, I've been in love with her for years," Tom said. "I'm going to ask for her hand in marriage right now."

"So am I," Dai said, jumping up. The two brothers set off, pushing and shoving each other all the way across the fields.

While they were still on their way, Sion came home, and he was horrified when his parents told him what had happened. He set off to Gwenllian's house at a run.

Tom and Dai reached Gwenllian's house together and they both knocked on the door.

"Sir," Tom said, when Gwenllian's father opened the door. "I wish to marry your daughter."

"No, he doesn't," Dai said. "I do."

Gwenllian's father looked at them both and scratched his head in puzzlement. "You'd better come indoors."

He showed them into the front parlour of the farmhouse: the best room, which was kept for special visitors. Gwenllian joined them a few minutes later, looking flustered and out of breath. She'd probably only just got back from her secret meeting with Sion, Tom thought with a nasty smile.

Gwenllian's father sat down. "So you two boys wish to marry my daughter. Obviously, you can't both marry her."

"I don't want to marry either of them," Gwenllian whispered, but her father took no notice.

"The man who marries Gwenllian will also inherit this farm when I die," he said. "I need to know you'll take care of it properly, and that you'll provide for Gwenllian and make her happy."

"I'll do all those things," Tom promised.

"So will I!" Dai said.

Just then, there was a banging on the door and Sion burst in, red-faced and sweaty from running. He had holes in his shirt from where he'd taken a shortcut through a bramble hedge, there were leaves in his hair and something that looked suspiciously like sheep droppings stuck to his left knee.

"Stop!" he panted. "I want to marry Gwenllian."

Everyone turned to stare at him.

"You?" his brothers sneered.

"You?" Gwenllian's father said, sounding surprised.

"You!" Gwenllian cried, her face lighting up. "Dad, I love Sion. He's the one I want to marry."

Her father put his hand up to stop her. "Hold on, now. You barely know Sion, how do you know you want to marry him? Look at the state of him!"

Gwenllian reddened. If she admitted she and Sean had been meeting in secret, she knew they'd be in big trouble. Her father didn't approve of secret meetings.

"Marriage is a serious business," her father said. "Your husband needs to be someone who'll work hard and take care of the farms. Someone who knows how to make a profit."

"Someone who doesn't mind getting his hands dirty," Gwenllian said with a pointed glance at Sion's muddy hands.

Her father frowned. "I've got an idea. Come outside, all of you."

He took them to the cowshed, where cows stood with their calves. He selected three brown calves, each one almost identical to the others. "These three were born on the same day," he said. "Take one each and look after it. At the end of the summer, take it to the fair to sell, and whoever makes the most money can marry Gwenllian."

Tom and Dai quickly seized two of the calves. The third one was maybe a little smaller, though there wasn't much in it. Casting a secret smile at Gwenllian, Sion led his calf out of the shed and took it home.

It wasn't long before Dai, the lazy brother, forgot all about his calf, and one day it escaped from the field and ran away. Tom looked after his calf well, but as the weeks passed, he could see that Sion's calf was even fatter and healthier. As the day of the fair approached, he became angrier and even meaner to Sion.

One night, Tom said he was going outside for a walk. The next morning, Sion went to check on his calf and found it lying on the ground in the cowshed, dead.

Sion's heart stopped in his chest. He dropped to his knees next to the calf and noticed a few black berries on the ground – yew berries. Yew was deadly poisonous to cattle.

Tom was waiting outside the cowshed, grinning, when Sion came out. "Bad luck," he said. "You should have taken better care of your calf."

He did it, Sion thought. Tom had poisoned the calf. But there was no way Sion could prove it. What could he do now?

Sadly, Sion went back into the cowshed and stood, looking down at the still body of the calf. Then he had an idea.

The day of the fair came. Tom's calf had grown into a fine young cow and, as he'd expected, he got a good price for it in the cattle auction, not that it mattered. Dai's calf had run away and Sion's had met with an unfortunate accident, so Tom had already won. Dai and Sion hadn't even bothered to come to the market.

Tom made his way back through the market stalls, jingling his purse of money and grinning to himself. At one point, he had to stop because a man in a ragged cloak and hood was selling shoelaces. He was joking and laughing with people and had gathered a big crowd around him. That was very inconsiderate, Tom thought, shoving his way through.

He soon forgot about the shoelace seller, though, because he had other things to think about, such as his marriage to Gwenllian and what to do about Dai and Sion. He couldn't have them hanging about the farm after he'd got married – especially not Sion.

That evening, Tom hurried across the valley to Gwenllian's house. He found a big crowd there, gathered together to celebrate the end of the fair. Tom set his purse of money down in front of Gwenllian's father. "Here," he said. "You don't need to count it. Dai's calf ran away and Sion's calf died. As you see, I'm the only one who earned anything at all."

Gwenllian let out a little cry. "Where is Sion?"

Tom shrugged. "He was too embarrassed to come and he decided he didn't want to marry you after all. But you don't need to worry: I'll be a good husband and I'll take care of both our farms."

Gwenllian's father tipped the money out of Tom's purse and stacked it up in little piles. "I'll announce the marriage tomorrow," he said, ignoring Gwenllian's unhappy face. "Gwenllian, fetch a chair for Tom, he's staying for supper."

But before Gwenllian could move, the door flew open and in marched a ragged-looking man wearing a tattered cloak and hood. It was the shoelace seller from the fair. What was he doing here?

"Do you mind?" Tom asked. "I'm just about to get engaged."

"That's what you think," the shoelace seller said, throwing back his hood. It was Sion.

"You!" Tom snarled.

"You?" Gwenllian's father said, confused.

"You!" Gwenllian cried, her face lighting up.

"You've got a cheek coming here," Tom said, "after you let your calf die."

Sion stared at him for a moment and then he turned to look at Gwenllian's father. "Yes, my calf died," he said. "Someone put yew leaves in the feeding trough. I don't know who would have been so cruel." He paused just long enough for Tom's cheeks to redden. "But," Sion went on, "the challenge you set us was to earn the most money for the calf. You didn't say how we had to do it. So I skinned my calf and I made shoelaces from the leather. Then, as many of you saw, I sold the laces for twopence a pair in the market today."

Lots of people looked down at the new laces in their shoes.

"Twopence a pair?" Tom scoffed. "You won't get very far with that!"

"Well," said Sion, "it depends on how many pairs there were." And he took a big bag of coins from underneath his cloak and emptied it on the table in front of Gwenllian's father.

Gwenllian's father looked at the mountain of

pennies and smiled. "That's the cleverest idea I've ever seen," he said. "And I bet it took you a lot of work too. That's exactly the kind of husband I want for my daughter. What do you think, Gwenllian?"

"Of course I want to marry Sion," Gwenllian said, her cheeks pink. "I've always wanted to marry him."

Tom stamped out of the house angrily while Sion joined the celebrations. A few months later, Sion and Gwenllian were married and they lived together very happily for the rest of their lives.

Taliesin Saves the Day

TALIESIN YN ACHUB Y DYDD

Taliesin, you may remember, was the greatest poet and storyteller who ever lived, and he had magical powers. "The Boy Who Asked Questions" told the story of Taliesin's birth. This story takes place thirteen years later.

Prince Taliesin was not happy. What was the point of being the most intelligent person in the kingdom of Ceredigion and speaking seventy-three languages, including the language of animals and birds, if his parents wouldn't listen to him?

"Father," he said, "I'm serious. If you go to King Maelgwn's palace this Christmas it will end badly."

Prince Elffin shook his head and laughed. "I'm not going to war, I'm going to a party. King Maelgwn will show off how rich he is and everyone will pretend to be impressed. We'll eat and drink and have fun and I'll be back before New Year. What could go wrong?"

Taliesin didn't know. He just had a bad feeling in his stomach. "Then let me come with you," he said.

Elffin put his hands on Taliesin's shoulders. "The invitation was for me, not for you. I need you to stay here and help your mother while I'm away."

He smiled, but he sounded impatient. Taliesin knew when to stop arguing. Maybe the feeling in his stomach was wrong for once. Like his father said, it was only a party.

Taliesin stood and watched as his father rode

away, then he went back inside the castle and waited for news, hoping it wouldn't be something terrible.

Meanwhile, Prince Elffin rode north to King Maelgwn's palace with a worried frown on his face. He loved his adopted son, and Taliesin had always brought him good luck. In fact, many years ago, Prince Elffin had been known as Elffin the Unlucky because nothing ever went right for him. Then one day he went to the lake to fish and he found a basket with a golden-haired child inside, and from the moment he'd brought the baby home, Elffin's luck had changed.

He hoped his luck wasn't about to turn bad again. But he couldn't very well turn down an invitation from the king, could he? And anyway, he'd been looking forward to the trip. Maelgwn was the richest king in Wales and he was famous for his parties.

As Elffin and his servants came within sight of Maelgwn's castle, the sound of singing filled the air and Elffin saw colourful banners waving on either side of the road to the castle.

King Maelgwn himself came striding to meet them as they got off their horses. "Elffin!" he shouted. "Come on in. The party's about to begin."

Elffin relaxed and smiled. Taliesin had been worrying about nothing. Leaving his servants to unpack his things, he followed the king through the castle to the great hall. Hundreds of people sat around the long tables, eating and drinking. The walls were covered with tapestries of Maelgwn riding into battle and slaying dragons. Elffin was very sure Maelgwn had never even seen a dragon, let alone slain one.

"What do you think?" Maelgwn shouted over the noise in the room.

Elffin looked up at the massive chandeliers, dripping wax from their fat candles, and he felt a sudden and very strange wave of homesickness for his quiet castle and small family. But Maelgwn was already pushing him to a table, and soon Elffin was squeezed in between two other princes and he didn't have time to feel homesick at all.

The week sped by in a blur of eating and drinking, horse-racing contests in the day and feasting every night. By the last night, Elffin's head ached and he was looking forward to going home the next day.

King Maelgwn stood up and banged on the table to get everyone's attention. "I've planned a special event for our last night."

At his words, trumpets sounded and acrobats

cartwheeled across the front of the hall where the servants had set up a stage.

"Lords and princes!" King Maelgwn announced. "Get ready for the greatest song contest ever. Twenty-five bards, chosen from every part of Wales, will perform for you, and you, the audience, will decide the winner."

Everyone cheered. Elffin joined in, though he was thinking that twenty-five bards would take a long time and he really wanted to go to bed.

The first bard stepped on to the stage. He was dressed all in white and held a harp that looked like it was made of silver.

What a shame Taliesin wasn't here, Elffin thought. The boy would have loved this.

The contest went on, bard after bard – and the costumes! One bard wore a glittering gold dress with a hat that looked like a cauldron. The next was all in black with shoes so high he appeared to float above the stage. Another sang while sitting on a horse and yet another swung from the ceiling on a rope. Elffin watched in a daze, his ears ringing with the cacophony of music and cheering.

Maelgwn strode over to join him. "What do you think?" the king shouted, slapping Elffin between the shoulders.

If Elffin's head hadn't been spinning quite so much, he'd have said that these were the best bards he'd ever heard in his life. You don't insult the king's entertainment, especially not at Christmas in front of everybody. But Elffin was tired from a week of non-stop parties and he was missing his home. The words came out of his mouth before his muddled brain knew what he was saying.

"They're not bad," he said. "But my own son Taliesin is better than all these bards put together."

As bad luck would have it, the bard onstage finished singing just as Elffin spoke and Elffin's word rang out across the suddenly quiet hall.

Everyone turned to stare and the people sitting around Elffin edged away from him nervously.

King Maelgwn's face set in a scowl. "So you think my entertainment is dull, do you?" he said. "Let's see what you think of my dungeon. Guards, lock him in the tower – and make sure you put plenty of chains on him."

That night in Ceredigion, Taliesin sat up in bed with a cry. He'd seen the whole thing, as vividly as if he'd been there himself – the bards, Maelgwn shouting, guards dragging Prince Elffin away.

Taliesin ran to his mother's room. "Wake up! Father's in trouble."

"Go back to sleep," his mother yawned. "You were dreaming."

But in the morning, Elffin's servants rode through the castle gates, and Elffin wasn't with them.

Panic spread through the castle. Maelgwn was famous for his parties, but he was also famous for his bad temper. He'd been known to lock people up and not let them go for years.

Taliesin was the only one who didn't panic. He'd been expecting something bad and he was prepared. He packed up a bag of clothes. "I'm going to King Maelgwn's palace," he said. "I know how to rescue Father."

Taliesin's mother looked down at him, her face tight with worry. Taliesin could tell what she was thinking. What could a boy do against a king? Taliesin took her hands. "I promise I'll be careful," he said. "I know what to do. I told you something bad would happen, didn't I?"

Finally, Taliesin's mother agreed as long as he promised to take some servants with him. "Take care," she said. "Ride straight to the palace and don't talk to any strangers on the way."

Taliesin set off. When he arrived at Maelgwn's palace, all the servants were talking about how Prince Elffin had insulted the king's bards. The bards were furious and the king had arranged for them all to perform again that night to make up for the insult.

Taliesin didn't say a word. When the time came for the evening feast, he made his way to the great hall. He saw the stage at the front of the hall and a door standing ajar next to it. That must be where the bards would come in, he thought. He made his way between the tables and sat down on the floor next to the door. Nobody took any notice of him.

Suddenly, the door next to Taliesin slammed back and a bard strutted through. He wore a green-and-pink-striped cloak and his hat was so wide he had to turn sideways to get through the door.

Everyone cheered except Taliesin. He flapped his index finger across his lips and made a noise that sounded like, *Blibber blabber!*

The bard swept on past without noticing the boy sitting on the floor. He mounted the steps to the stage, threw out his arms and opened his mouth wide to sing.

He paused. "*Blibber blabber*," he said.

The bard stopped in confusion, cleared his throat loudly and tried again.

"*Blibber blabber*."

"What's going on?" Maelgwn shouted. "Why aren't you singing?"

"*Blibber blabber*," said the bard.

The next bard pushed his way into the hall. This one had a gold cloak covered in glittering stars.

"*Blibber blabber*," Taliesin whispered.

The bard jumped up onstage. "Stand aside: I'll show you how it's done." A strange look crossed his face. "*Blibber blabber*."

Some people in the audience started to laugh. Maelgwn's face turned red. Taliesin could see he didn't like being laughed at.

"Throw these two clowns off the stage," Maelgwn said. "Call in the rest of the bards."

The other bards all rushed in together. As each one brushed past Taliesin, he flapped his lips and made the same noise.

"*Blibber blabber*," the bards all said.

"What are you doing?" Maelgwn bellowed at them. The bards cleared their throats and coughed and gargled with water, but every time they opened their mouths to speak, they made the same noise.

One of the bards fainted in terror. Maelgwn banged his fist on the table until all the plates jumped.

"Will someone tell me what's going on?"

Everyone was quiet. Taliesin stood up from his corner. "I can tell you," he said. "Your bards are all big-headed. They think they're the best, but they're not."

"*Blibber blabber*," the bards shouted angrily.

"You're just a boy," Maelgwn snapped. "Who do you think you are?"

"I was a baby set adrift in a basket," Taliesin said. He took a step toward the stage. "I was a seed of corn, I was a crow and a fish and a hare." He climbed the steps to the stage. "I was Gwion Bach, who loved questions, and now I am Taliesin, son of Elffin, and his bard."

And then Taliesin began to sing. He sang about a boy and a witch. He sang about a magical battle across land and lake and sky. He sang about a hen who pecked up a seed of corn. His voice carried to every corner of the great hall and everyone listened with their mouths open. The boy's music was like birdsong and sunlight. One moment the notes skipped like a breeze across water, the next they softened and filled with the warmth of summer. By the time the last note faded, half the audience was weeping – including the bards.

Taliesin stopped singing. "If any of your bards think they can out-sing me," he said, "let them try." He snapped his fingers. At once the bards found they could speak again, but none of them challenged him. They all edged back on the stage, leaving Taliesin standing at the front, alone.

Then Taliesin sang another song: a hard, angry song about a king who locked a man in a tower. The great hall of the castle trembled. The chandeliers swung in circles overhead, the tapestries of Maelgwn's imaginary exploits shook loose from their holdings and crashed to the floor. The bards fled, while the princes and lords tried to hide under the tables.

Maelgwn knew when he was beaten. "Fetch Prince Elffin," he ordered.

His guards dashed out of the room and returned in less than a minute, dragging a bewildered-looking Elffin, still loaded down with chains.

"Hello, Father," Taliesin sang.

Elffin's chains rattled and fell off.

"I told you you'd get into trouble, coming here

without me," Taliesin said.

"So you did," Elffin said. He looked around at the frightened bards, the collapsed tapestries and Maelgwn the king, whose face was dark with anger, but who didn't dare say a word. Elffin didn't know what had happened, but he made a silent promise to always take his son's advice in the future. He thought of his own quiet castle by the sea and he smiled. "Let's go home," he said.

Pryderi and the Fairy Queen

Pryderi a Brenhines y Tylwyth Teg

Pryderi, you may remember, was the son of Prince Pwyll and Princess Rhiannon. He grew up to have many adventures. This is one of the strangest. You will find it, along with his other adventures, in the Mabinogion.

Pryderi, son of Pwyll, grew up to be just like his father. He was brave, he liked to have his friends around him, and he sometimes listened to his friends when he really shouldn't.

Sadly, Prince Pwyll died, and Pryderi became the new Prince of Dyfed. He soon found out that being in charge wasn't as much fun as he'd imagined. People kept asking him to decide things when all he wanted to do was to spend his time with his friends. Pryderi's best friend was called Manawydan. In fact, they were such good friends that Pryderi invited Manawydan to stay with him so they could spend all their time together, with hunting and fishing in the day and feasting in the evening. And, though Pryderi's mother scolded him for neglecting his duties as the new ruler, Pryderi wouldn't listen to her.

One day they were having supper in the castle hall. The great room was full of people and noise. A hundred people sat at long tables while, around them, servants ran to and fro, carrying plates. A group of musicians played in one corner, and dogs barked, fighting over scraps of meat.

Suddenly, in the middle of all this, came a great peal of thunder. A white mist came down over everything, pouring through the castle windows and filling the rooms so that the two friends could barely see each other across the table.

The mist cleared just as suddenly as it had come. Pryderi and Manawydan looked at each other across the empty table, in the empty, silent hall.

"Where is everyone?" Pryderi asked. He looked under the table in case they'd all hidden, but underneath the table was empty too. He ran to the window and looked out. The fields around the castle, which should be full of people, were empty. Even the sheep had vanished.

"What's happening?" Manawydan asked, his voice trembling.

Pryderi shook his head. This was a mystery.

The two friends searched the whole castle and found nobody. They went outside and looked in every field and every house. No people, no animals, nothing. Only their two horses stamping restlessly in the stable. That was stranger than anything – why should their horses still be here when every other animal had disappeared?

"You know what this means, don't you?" Manawydan asked.

"Yes," Pryderi said. "We need to find out what has happened and get everyone back."

"Well, we could do that," Manawydan said, "or we could enjoy ourselves for a while. We have the whole of Wales to ourselves, and I'm sure everyone will turn up again if we wait."

Pryderi wasn't so sure. This was some sort of evil enchantment, he thought. He wished he'd paid more attention when his mother had talked about the magical Otherworld. "All right," he agreed. "Let's wait." He couldn't think of anything else to do.

The two friends waited for a whole year. They soon found out that, though all the animals had disappeared from farms and homes, the forests were still full of wild animals, the rivers and lakes full of fish. The friends spent their time hunting and fishing just like they had before everyone vanished. At the end of the year, Pryderi was bored. He missed his family and other friends and, though he'd never admit it, he was getting a bit fed up of only having Manawydan to talk to.

"We need to do something," he said one evening as he and Manawydan sat in the empty castle hall.

"I agree," Manawydan said. "Let's go to England. We can get jobs and pretend to be ordinary people. It'll be fun."

That wasn't exactly what Pryderi had in mind, but Manawydan started talking about England as if they'd already agreed to go, and Pryderi didn't know what else to do.

The next day, they packed up their clothes and rode off, leaving Wales behind. The first town they arrived at was Hereford. Looking at the bustling streets, Pryderi felt strange. He hadn't seen anyone apart from Manawydan for a whole year and he hadn't realized how much he'd missed the people of Wales until now.

"What jobs shall we do?" he asked Manawydan.

Manawydan got off his horse and rested his arms on his saddle. "I know! Let's be saddlemakers. We spend so much time riding, we should know all about saddles."

So the two friends rented a shop, bought a stock of leather and started making saddles. Manawydan turned out to be surprisingly good at it – so good, in fact, that people only wanted to buy saddles from him, and all the other saddlemakers in Hereford lost their customers.

The saddlemakers came to the shop. "Pack up your things and leave," they said. "If you stay one more day, we will make you sorry."

"How dare they tell us to leave?" Pryderi said. "We should fight them all and teach them a lesson."

"But then we'd end up in prison," Manawydan said, being sensible for once. "I'm getting bored with saddles anyway. Let's move to another town and make shields."

"Can you make shields?" Pryderi grumbled.

"I expect so. I've never tried."

The following morning the friends left Hereford and rode on to Worcester, where they opened a shield-making shop. It turned out that Manawydan could make shields. In fact, he did it so well that very soon all the other shieldmakers in the town formed an angry crowd outside the shop and ordered them to leave.

This time, Manawydan wanted to stay and fight, but Pryderi persuaded him it was time to move on. "Let's be shoemakers," he said. "Shoemakers don't know how to fight, they won't cause us any trouble."

They left town that very night and rode to the next town, where they set up a shoe-making shop.

Soon, they were making the best shoes in the county. The other shoemakers were furious, but as Pryderi guessed, none of them knew how to fight. So they hired all the saddlemakers from Hereford and all the shieldmakers from Worcester and they formed a great crowd outside Pryderi and Manawydan's shop.

"I didn't expect them to do that," Pryderi said, listening to the angry shouting. "Can we please go back to Wales and find out what happened to everyone?"

Manawydan peeped out through the window. It was a very big crowd outside. "I think you may be right," he said. "It's time to go home."

They set off the next day and soon crossed the border into empty Wales. They returned to Pryderi's castle and every day they rode out across the land, looking for the lost people.

Soon, Manawydan grew bored. "When everyone comes back, they'll be hungry," he said. "I'm going to grow some food for them."

Pryderi was becoming less sure that everyone would come back. He wished he could be like his friend and not worry about these things, but he was starting to believe that this whole situation was somehow his fault. It was the prince's job to protect everyone, after all. If he'd done his job properly, maybe everyone would still be here.

While Pryderi kept looking for the lost people,

Manawydan planted three fields of wheat and, though he'd never grown anything before, he turned out to be good at it. The wheat shot up, straight and tall, shining like pure gold in the summer sun. Manawydan was very proud of them.

Then one morning, he came into the castle in a towering rage. "Someone has stolen one of my fields of wheat!"

How could someone steal an entire field? Pryderi wondered, but when he went to look, he saw that one of the fields was a mess of brown stubble and broken stalks and not a single ear of wheat remained.

"Could it be slugs?" Pryderi asked. He didn't know much about gardening.

Manawydan didn't know much about gardening either. "I'm bored of growing wheat," he said. "Never mind, we've still got two fields left. I'll reap one of them tomorrow."

"You could do it now," Pryderi suggested. "Before it's all taken." But Manawydan's mind had already moved on to other things.

The next day, Manawydan stamped into the castle, yelling, "The second field has all gone!"

Pryderi resisted the urge to say *I told you so.* "Why

don't we sit out in the last field tonight," he suggested, "and then we can see what's happening?"

Manawydan agreed, and that night the two friends packed a picnic basket with food and drink, and camped out in the field.

All was quiet for several hours, but as midnight approached, Pryderi heard the sound of scurrying feet and hundreds of squeaking voices.

Mice! Hundreds and hundreds of mice. They rushed into the field in a brown wave, running up the wheat stalks and nibbling off the ears.

Pryderi and Manawydan yelled and stamped, trying to frighten them away, but it was no good. Within a few minutes, every ear of wheat was bitten off, and the mice were running out of the field, carrying the ears on their backs.

Manawydan dived after one fat mouse and caught her in both hands.

"You little thief!" he shouted. "I'm going to hang you for this."

"You're going to hang a mouse?" Pryderi asked. "For stealing wheat?"

"Yes!" Manawydan shouted, too angry to listen. "Where's that picnic basket?"

He took out all the knives and forks, then he

pushed the mouse into the basket and slammed the lid shut. Then he started tying the knives and forks together to make a tiny cutlery gallows. Pryderi watched, trying not to laugh.

But then Pryderi heard something – horse's hooves. He looked up and saw a man riding across the field towards them.

Pryderi leaped up. It had been years since he'd seen anyone in Wales, except for Manawydan.

The man got off his horse. "What are you doing?" he asked.

Manawydan scowled. "We're hanging a thief." He took the mouse out of the picnic basket and held it up.

"It's not right to hang a mouse," the stranger said. "Let it go and I'll pay you twenty pounds."

Twenty pounds was quite a lot of money. A suspicion stirred in Pryderi's mind. "What's the good of money when everyone has disappeared?" he asked. "No, thanks, we'll hang the mouse."

The stranger looked a little alarmed. "All right, then: fifty pounds."

Pryderi folded his arms. "Why are you so worried about a mouse?"

The stranger sighed. "Because," he said, "that

mouse is my wife. "My name is Llwyd and I am an enchanter. I cast the spell over Wales and took everyone away into the Otherworld."

"But why?" asked Manawydan.

"Because of what Pryderi's father did," Llwyd said. "Lord Gwawl wanted to marry Princess Rhiannon, but Prince Pwyll tricked him."

Pryderi had heard the story many times. Pwyll had trapped Gwawl in a magic bag and threatened to leave him there for ever unless he promised that Rhiannon could marry Pwyll.

"Rhiannon made Gwawl promise not to take revenge on her or Pwyll," Llwyd said, "and so he asked me to take revenge on you instead. How does it feel to be prince of nobody?"

Pryderi looked around the empty field. It felt lonely, he thought.

The mouse wriggled out of Manawydan's grip and turned into a lady. "We saw you were growing food and we knew you'd be angry if we took it all, so we did. Can we go now?"

"Not until you break the enchantment and put Wales back to normal," Pryderi said. "And you have to promise never to bother us again."

Llwyd sighed and raised his hands. Thunder

rumbled and a white mist descended over the fields. When it cleared, Llwyd and his wife were gone. But Pryderi heard cows mooing close by, a sheep baaed, and as the sun rose, he saw smoke rising from the chimneys of houses. All of Wales was back as it had been before.

The Afanc

Yr Afanc

The River Conwy is twenty-seven miles long, stretching all the way from the moors of the Snowdonia National Park to the sea at Conwy Bay. There are many little pools and tributaries along the way, and one of these is called Llyn-yr-Afanc – Lake of the Afanc. This is why.

Once upon a time, Wales was a land of magic and monsters. Every mountain had its dragon, the forests rang with the songs of the Tylwyth Teg, and every river, lake and swamp was home to some strange creature. Then the first humans ventured into the land. They mined the mountains for iron and copper, they cut down trees to build houses, they fished in the rivers and they drained the swamps to create farms.

The old inhabitants of Wales withdrew into the shadows. The dragons burrowed deep into caves and fell asleep. The Tylwyth Teg hid themselves among the remaining forests. The creatures of the rivers swam out to sea – but a few remained, lurking in the mud and watching the humans with hungry eyes.

The most fearsome of these creatures was called the Afanc. It looked a bit like a crocodile and a bit like a bear, a bit like an elephant and a bit like a shark. It coiled in a pool next to the River Conwy, enjoying the feel of the cool water on its scales and waiting. If any animal happened to stray a little too close to the pool, if any bird rested on the water, even for a second, then . . .

SNAP. The Afanc had them.

Very soon there was little living around the pool and the Afanc lay hungry, waiting for new prey.

And then the humans arrived.

They were a small group, only ten families at first. They stopped their horses and carts on the flat green land between the forest and the river. They were already imagining farms and houses here.

One girl tugged nervously at her father's hand.

"I don't like it," she said. "There are no birds singing. And there ought to be fish in that pond. I can't see any."

"Hush, Becca," her father said. "The fish are probably hiding." He looked back at the mountain slopes and his fingers twitched. Becca knew he was already imagining his own blacksmith's forge, turning iron into horseshoes and tools for the farms which would grow up.

The families set up camp and very soon they were chopping wood, lighting fires and planning their new town.

Deep in the lake, the Afanc heard their voices and its mouth watered so hard its saliva created little whirlpools. It didn't move – not yet. It knew that when these strange new creatures arrived in a place, there would soon be more and more of them. The Afanc was patient. It would wait.

A month went by, and then another. More families moved in to join the town. They built little houses to replace their old tents. Becca's father was busy hammering iron all day. Becca still didn't feel happy here. With no one her own age to talk to, she spent her time listening instead.

She liked to hear the rattle of rain on the roof when she lay in bed. She loved the clang of her father's hammers, and the sizzle of red-hot iron plunging into water to cool. Often, she sat at the edge of the forest and listened to the wind singing, and if she listened hard, she was sure she could hear other, not-quite-human voices singing from tree to tree.

Be careful, the voices seemed to be saying. *There is danger here.*

One day, one of the townsmen took his fishing rod down to the deep pool of water beside the river.

Beneath the water, the Afanc stirred. The hairs in its nostrils twitched eagerly and trails of green saliva dripped from its jaws to mix with the water around. It had waited long enough and now it was hungry. The Afanc stretched, flicked its tail and swam up through the water.

The fisherman saw the ripples in the pool and thought he'd found a fish. But then he saw a pair of eyes, each one as big as his head, and a long brown snout, covered with bristles and tusks. The fisherman had just enough time to yell in terror before the Afanc's jaws snapped shut on him.

When the fisherman didn't come home, people thought he might have been killed by a wild animal in the forest. Or he'd got bored here and decided to move on: people did that sometimes. Some of the men went out to the forest to look, but they found nothing. Nobody thought to check the pool by the river because it looked so calm and peaceful.

It wasn't until the fourth person disappeared and someone found a broken fishing rod by the pool that everyone realized the truth. But now, the Afanc was bolder. More people vanished, and cattle too. Some nights, the people in the town would hear the monster roaring. Some mornings, if the Afanc didn't swallow its prey whole, there would be bones floating in the pool.

The whole town came together for a meeting. Becca went with her father and sat in the back row and listened, a frown on her face.

The monster was a great alligator. No, it was a

giant walrus. It was an elephant, or a bear. Nobody could agree. One thing they did agree on, though: if the people wanted to be safe in their homes, they had to kill it.

Finally, the mayor stood up. "We'll go to the pool tomorrow," he said. "Everyone must take a weapon – a spear or a sword, or whatever you have."

"It won't work," Becca whispered. "The creature comes from ancient times. I've heard the Fair Folk singing about it. You can't kill magical creatures with ordinary weapons."

Her father was the only person who heard her and he shook his head at her, warning her to be quiet.

The next day, all the townsmen gathered at the edge of the pool. The Afanc surged out of the water towards them. Its head was flat and leathery, and tusks sprouted from its bristly snout. It had a long brown body, covered in scales, with a ridge of sharp spines along its back. Its tail ended in a bony spike which it swung back and forth.

The men scattered, screaming. The Afanc roared. This was fun! It bounded after the humans, trying to decide which one to eat next. The men threw their spears and shot their arrows but every weapon bounced off the monster's scales.

The men fled back to town. "The monster cannot be killed," they said. "We must pack up our homes and move before it eats us all."

Becca's frown deepened. She didn't want to be eaten, but they'd built their homes here now. The first crops of the season were growing in the field. If they moved, they'd have to leave everything behind, and where would they get food for the winter?

She thought for a while and then she got up and walked quietly into the forest.

"Hello," she called. "I need your help."

An hour or two later, Becca walked back to the town, feeling a little unsteady.

"I know what the monster is," she said. "It's called the Afanc and it's the last one living in Wales. It's a fairy creature and it cannot be harmed by any human weapon. But song will tame it and iron will bind it."

Nobody wanted to listen to her – especially not her father. "I can't have you fighting monsters," he said. "It's too dangerous. Better that we pack up our things and find somewhere else to live."

"Please, Father," Becca said. "If we don't stop the Afanc, it will keep killing people and it will grow until it fills the whole river. Nobody will be safe. I'm not afraid." That was a lie – she was terrified at the thought of the monster, but the fairy people in the forest had told her what to do and she trusted them. "I'm not going to fight the monster," she said. "I'll sing it to sleep. The rest of you will have to do the dangerous part."

Finally, after a lot of arguing, the people agreed to try Becca's plan. Her father set to work making iron chains. He used every bit of iron in the town and then he sent people out to the nearby towns to buy even more iron. When he'd finished, he had a length of chain that was so heavy it took fifty people to lift it.

"Ready?" he asked Becca.

She nodded, trying to hide the trembling in her knees. "Ready."

She led the way to the river.

The people huddled together, terrified. Was that a pair of green eyes peering at them across the pond-weed? Was that creaking just the wind in the trees or was it the sound of a pair of jaws slowly opening?

Becca drew in a deep breath and began to sing.

She sang one of the lullabies her father used to sing her when she was little. At first her voice was thin and frightened and she stumbled over the words, but she finished the first verse and felt braver.

She stepped a little closer to the pool, her voice rising and falling on the breeze.

Deep in the pool, the Afanc snapped its mouth shut in amazement. It had never heard anyone sing before. Usually, people just said, "Arrrrgh!" But this was beautiful. There was something magical in the sound. It reminded the Afanc of a time when Wales was wild and free, when dragons roamed the mountains.

The Afanc rose to the surface of the pool, its slimy green eyes fixed on the small human who was making such a marvellous noise.

The townspeople all held their breath, and Becca kneeled down on the grass – she had to because her legs were shaking too much for her to stand.

The Afanc crept out of the water and lay down in front of her, and then it rolled over on to its back and waved its horrible feet in the air, just like a cat wanting to have its belly rubbed.

Still singing, Becca reached out and scratched the monster under the chin. Its scales felt cold and rough. The Afanc closed its eyes and made a strange noise, like rocks falling. Becca realized what it was – the Afanc was purring.

She started the lullaby again and sang it all the way through to the end. The Afanc began to snore.

The townspeople crept forward and started to wrap the monster up in the iron chain from its nose right down to the tip of its tail.

As soon as they'd finished, Becca stopped singing and ran back out of the way.

The Afanc woke. The beautiful sound had vanished and now it was hungry. It tried to leap to its feet, but its feet were wrapped in heavy iron and it fell over. Furious, it thrashed and roared. It rolled back and forth on the riverbank, tearing up great chunks of earth, but it couldn't escape. Eventually it flopped down, exhausted.

Then the people brought in their strongest oxen, yoked them together and fastened the end of the chain to the yoke. Slowly, because the Afanc was very heavy, they began to walk. They dragged the raging monster away from the river, across the fields, up and down hills until, on the eastern slope of Mount Snowden, they found a lake of dark water standing all on its own. The people unfastened the Afanc from the oxen and heaved it in, chains and all. It hit the water with a great splash and sank out of sight.

The people went home and the Afanc never bothered them again.

You can still find the lake on Mount Snowden. It's called Llyn Glaslyn. Nobody has ever seen the Afanc, but if you happen to visit the lake, don't go too close to the water, and always sing a lullaby, just in case.

King Arthur's Cave

Ogof Brenin Arthur

Did you know that King Arthur lived in Wales? Geoffrey of Monmouth, who wrote a history of Britain, said that King Arthur's court of Camelot was actually the South Wales town of Caerleon.

According to another legend, somewhere in mid-Wales, you can find the footprint of Arthur's favourite dog, and there are several lakes in Snowdonia which are supposed to contain Arthur's sword, Excalibur. There are many other stories too.

Wales is full of legends and you never know when you might stumble into one . . .

This story happened only yesterday.

Stephen had been looking forward to the holiday in Wales until he realized two things. First, there was no mobile signal anywhere around the cottage. And second, whenever Stephen went out exploring, he had to take his little sister, Emily, with him.

It wasn't that Stephen didn't like Emily. He did. She was funny, and she was great at coming up with imaginary games to play. But she was three years younger than him and a lot smaller, so Stephen, who really wanted to explore the mountains, had to keep stopping and waiting for her to catch up with him. And also she had a habit of stopping and staring about, and Stephen couldn't persuade her to come on until she'd seen everything.

She was doing it now, standing with her head to one side, gazing at some old tree that was growing at an angle out of a rock.

"It's only a tree," Stephen said, starting to feel annoyed. He'd wanted to climb to the top of the mountain today, but Emily had spotted a track leading off the main path and she'd insisted on following it to see what was there. This was it: rocks in front of them and the tree stuck out almost sideways, its spindly branches looking as if they might drop off at any moment. He climbed up to it and tugged one of the bottom branches. It snapped cleanly off in his hand.

"Stephen!" Emily said.

"What? It's only a branch." He jumped down and swished the stick through the grass, pretending that he was a knight and the stick was a sword. "Can we go somewhere else now, or do you want to carry on staring?"

He walked away, swinging the stick. He hoped that Emily would come running after him, and she did. They squeezed back along the narrow track and climbed the bank that they'd slid down earlier.

Then, as they climbed the path that led up the mountain, they saw a boy. He had black hair and green eyes and he appeared so suddenly on the path it was as if he'd stepped out of the air.

"Hello," Emily said. "I'm Emily and this is my brother, Stephen. Are you on holiday?"

"I live here," the boy said.

There wasn't a house in sight. Obviously, he meant he lived somewhere close by, Stephen thought. He dug his stuck into the ground and leaned on it. The boy's gaze sharpened.

"Where did you get that?"

Stephen felt oddly guilty. He hadn't seen any signs saying they couldn't take bits off trees, but he might have missed them. "It's only a stick," he said. "There was a half-dead tree growing out of a rock back there."

The boy eyed him up and down. "Can you remember where it is?" he asked. "Can you show me?"

Why did he want to see an old tree? Stephen knew not to talk to strangers, but that was grown-up strangers, not other boys. "We probably need to get back to the cottage," he said uncertainly.

"No, we don't," Emily said. "We've got loads of time."

The boy smiled. "Tell you what, show me where you found the tree and I'll show you something so wonderful you'll never forget it."

He was making that up, Stephen thought. But Emily danced from foot to foot with excitement. Stephen sighed. "All right," he said. "But we can't be long."

He led the way back down the path and on to the narrow track they'd found. They pushed their way through the long grass and brambles until they came back to the place where the tree stood, sticking out of a rock.

The boy gave a low cry and scrambled up the rock, then he dropped to his hands and knees and started digging in the loose earth around the tree roots. Stephen stared. What was the boy doing? Did he want to dig up the whole tree?

Emily climbed up after the boy. "I can see a hole," she said.

Stephen started to tell her not to be silly, but when he climbed up, he saw that she was right. The tree roots clutched at the rook, but between them there was a gap that seemed to go on right into the rocks behind.

They all started to dig and soon they'd made a hole big enough to crawl inside. The boy wriggled in first. Emily crawled after him eagerly. Stephen followed, his heart beating hard.

A moment later, Emily stopped, and Stephen stopped too. His mouth fell open at what he saw.

It should have been dark underground, but they were in a cavern flooded with golden light. Lying on the stone floor all around were men in armour. They lay on their backs and each one had a sword and a shield at his side. Silver and gold coins spilled out of the remains of mouldy bags.

At the far end of the cavern, a man, bigger than

all the others, sat on a stone throne, a sword resting across his knees.

They must be statues, Stephen thought, although the knights looked far too real to be statues. They looked as if they were sleeping.

"What is this place?" he whispered. "Who are they?" His voice was far too loud in the silent cavern and he shrank back.

The boy dropped to his knees and started filling his pockets with coins. "The man on the throne is King Arthur. Around him lie his knights. They are waiting for Britain's hour of greatest need, when they will wake and take up their weapons once again to fight."

The thought sent a cold shiver through Stephen. He gazed around in amazement. The boy was right – this was a wonder he'd never forget.

The boy, however, only seemed to care about the silver and gold. He crawled around the sleeping knights, grabbing up handful after greedy handful. When his pockets were full, he stuffed gold coins into his shirt.

"Stop," Stephen said. "Put it back. This doesn't belong to us."

"It belongs to me now," the boy said. He shot

Stephen a glare so fierce that Stephen didn't dare argue. Then Emily nudged him.

"Stephen, look."

Stephen turned and saw a golden bell hanging from the wall. Beneath it was a silver plaque, engraved with words in a strange language. He pushed the bell gently.

He hadn't expected it to move, but it swung and a note rang out through the cave. The ground trembled. Emily clutched Stephen's arm. All around, the knights stirred. Armoured hands reached for swords.

King Arthur's eyes opened and he sat up straight on his throne. "Who rang the bell?" he asked. "Is it time?"

Stephen's breath caught in his chest. He opened his mouth to speak, but before he could say a word, a voice echoed through the cavern. "No, it is just a greedy fairy boy and two human children who didn't know any better. Sleep on, Arthur the Great, your day has not yet come."

King Arthur's head dropped forward in sleep. One by one, his knights let go of their swords and settled back on the ground. Within seconds, all was quiet again.

“That was really stupid,” the boy hissed. He grabbed Stephen and Emily by the hands and dragged them out of the cave.

Stephen stood, blinking, in the sunshine. Had that really happened? He turned to ask the boy, but the boy had vanished.

Emily hugged herself. “We saw King Arthur! We have to tell Mum and Dad.”

They ran back to the cottage, bursting with the news. Of course, Mum and Dad thought they were making up stories.

“We can show you where the cave is,” Stephen insisted.

But when they took their parents up the mountain path, they couldn’t find the little winding track, or the rocks with the tree. It was as if the cave had never been there.

It is still there, though, somewhere. Next time you’re in the Welsh mountains, look out for a narrow path that leads down a steep bank. Maybe you’ll find a tree growing out of a rock with a cave underneath. Maybe you’ll be the one to wake King Arthur.

Other books in the Scholastic classics collection...

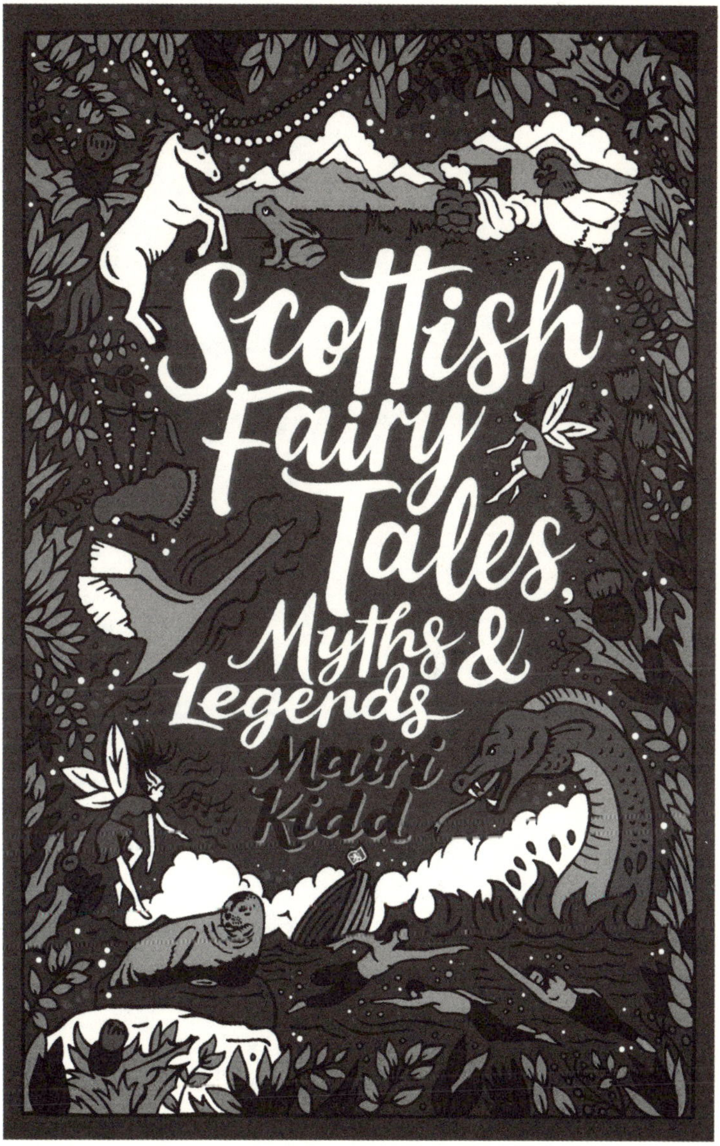
Scottish
Fairy
Tales,
Myths &
Legends
Mairi
Kidd

100 QUESTIONS

THE HUMAN BODY

AND ALL THE ANSWERS TOO!

RobinAge
India's Favourite Newspaper for Children

SCHOLASTIC
New York Toronto London Auckland
Sydney New Delhi Hong Kong

Published by Scholastic India Pvt. Ltd.
A subsidiary of Scholastic Inc., New York, 10012 (USA).
Publishers since 1920, with international operations in Canada, Australia, New Zealand, the United Kingdom, India, and Hong Kong.

For information regarding permission, write to:
Scholastic India Pvt. Ltd.
A-27, Ground Floor, Sigma Centre
Infocity-1, Sector 34, Gurgaon-122001 (India)

First Printing: 2020

This reprint edition: February 2026

ISBN- 978-93-90189-08-3

Printed in India at MicroPrints India, New Delhi

CONTENTS

THE BIG BRAIN 1

SENSATIONAL SENSES 11

OUR ARMOUR 25

THE HEALTHY HEART 35

DIGEST THIS! 43

STRONG BONES, MIGHTY MUSCLES! 53

THE AMAZING HUMAN BODY! 65

GLOSSARY 88

THE BIG BRAIN

What is the brain made of?

The brain is made up of three main parts—the cerebrum, which is divided into two chambers and controls speech, emotions, intelligence and more; the cerebellum, which controls movement and coordination; and the brain stem that connects the brain to the spinal cord.

The brain also has two smaller parts called the diencephalon, which transmits sensory information, and the pituitary gland, which controls the release of hormones in the body.

The brain is composed of sixty per cent fat and the rest is protein with some muscle tissue in the blood vessels that supply the brain. The protein element in the brain is found in the neurons. There are approximately eighty-six billion neurons in the brain.

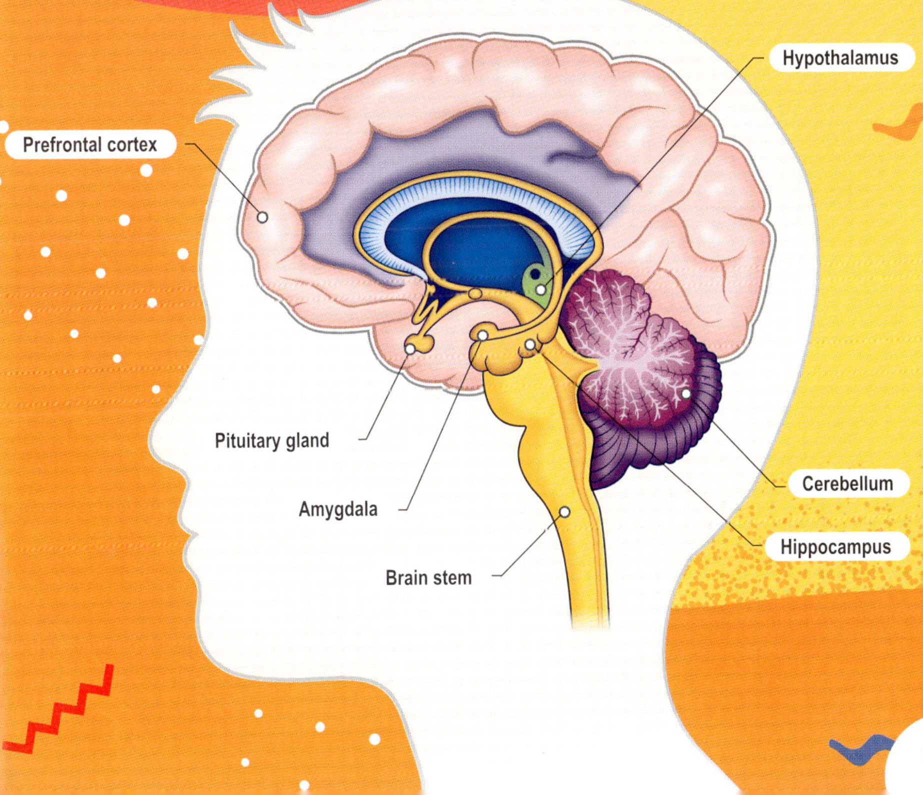

How big is the human brain?

The average human brain usually makes up about two per cent of the entire body weight, which means it weighs approximately 1.4 kg. The average brain measures 14 cm in width, 16 cm in length and 9 cm in height.

At birth, the human brain is only half its adult size, but contains all the neurons it will ever possess. The brain develops fastest from birth to the age of three. Although men have slightly larger brains than women, certain regions of women's brains are better-developed. For instance, the part of the brain that is related to learning and memory is larger in women.

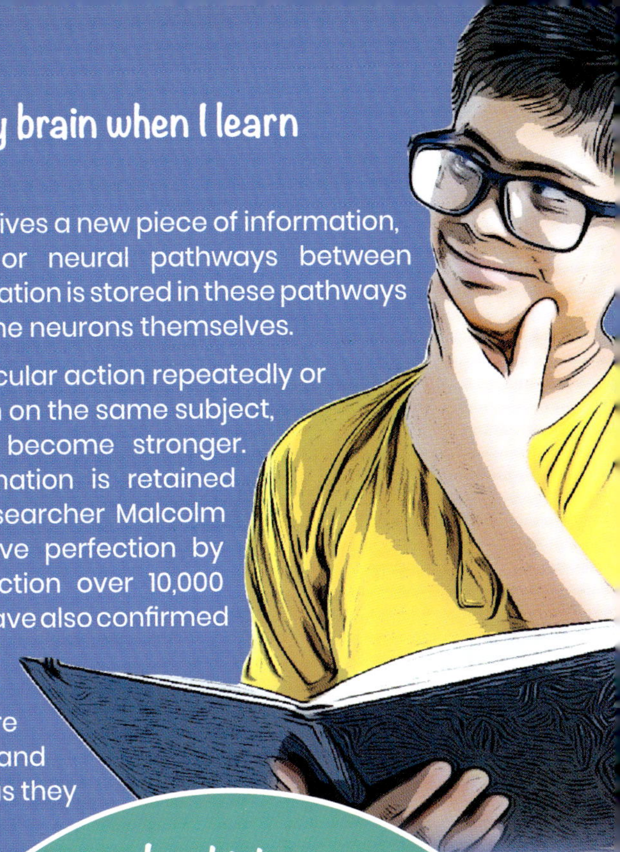

What happens in my brain when I learn something new?

Each time the brain receives a new piece of information, it forms connections or neural pathways between neurons. The new information is stored in these pathways or networks and not in the neurons themselves.

Each time we do a particular action repeatedly or receive new information on the same subject, the related pathways become stronger. As a result, the information is retained better. According to researcher Malcolm Gladwell, people achieve perfection by repeating the same action over 10,000 hours. Neuroscientists have also confirmed that the brain does not stop learning at any age. Adults' brains are constantly growing and reshaping themselves as they learn new things.

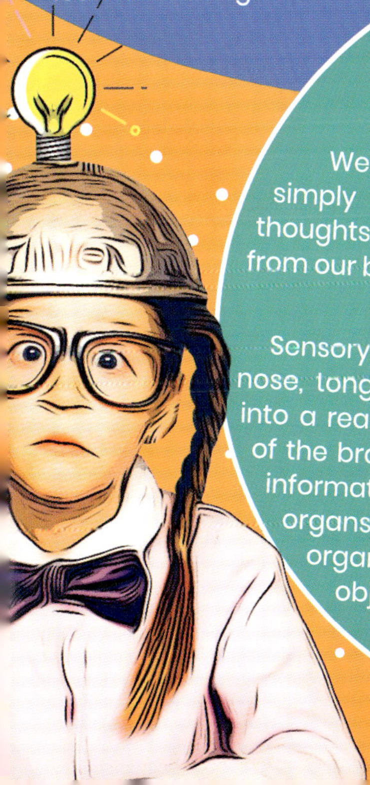

In which part of the brain do thoughts occur?

We think all the time, but our thoughts don't simply pop up inside our heads. Instead, our thoughts are the result of signals that travel to and from our brain across a network that flows through our entire body.

Sensory data is sent to the brain from the eyes, ears, nose, tongue and skin. The brain turns these signals into a reaction that we call thoughts. Different parts of the brain are used to put together or gather the information that is sent from the different sense organs. So, we can say that the brain is just an organ that processes external events and objects and generates a response. These events and objects are known as stimuli.

Does the brain feel pain?

To feel pain, an organ needs to have pain receptors called nociceptors. There are close to 200 pain receptors on every square centimetre of the skin, and these receptors alert the brain and spinal cord to pain. The brain lacks these pain receptors and hence cannot feel pain.

The scalp, the covering around the brain and the covering around the skull bones have pain receptors and can feel pain. For example, when we experience a headache, it is actually the structures that comprise the head—scalp nerves, muscles, blood vessels, facial nerves and neck nerves—that have a problem and cause pain. The headache could be caused by restricted blood flow or compression of nerves.

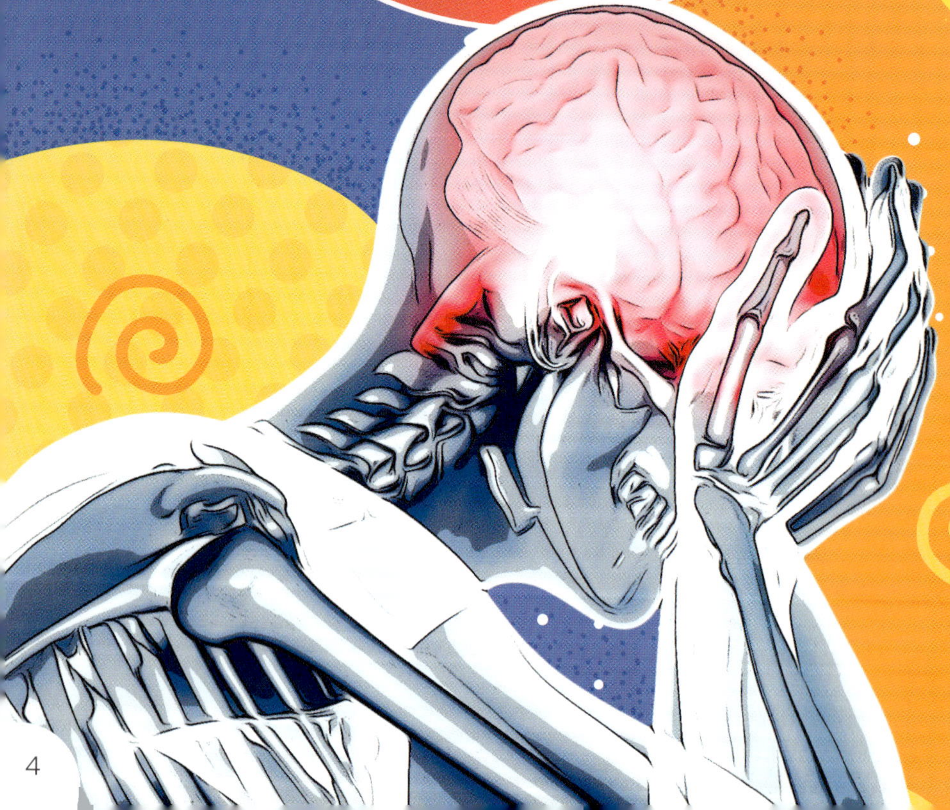

Why can't I remember things I did as a baby?

A phenomenon called childhood amnesia is the reason why most people cannot remember being a child. Although children aged three years can remember most of their past, by the time they reach the age of nine, this memory decreases to only about thirty-five per cent of what they could remember at the age of three.

Some scientists say that the way memories are formed changes as we grow. When a child is about eight or nine, he or she begins to store memories based on when and where they occurred. It is believed that this causes the brain to cut off or delete memories from earlier years while focusing on specific details of more recent memories. This is called retrieval-induced forgetting (RIF).

Another explanation suggests that infants don't have a sense of self, which is needed to develop memories about things that happened to them. This is also known as autobiographical memory. And so, babies find it difficult to pick out the things that were personally relevant and don't remember their past.

What happens to my brain during meditation?

During meditation, the brain becomes calmer and enters a state of deep relaxation. The level of the hormone cortisol, which is released when a person is stressed, reduces. The frontal lobe of the brain, which is responsible for emotions and awareness of oneself, stops processing too much information. The parietal lobe of the brain, which processes information gathered by our sense organs, slows down. Meditation increases the grey matter in the brain, which is responsible for learning and memory. The brain also produces alpha and theta waves, which are usually produced when you are sleeping.

Why do people yawn?

When our body is tired, it takes in less oxygen because our breathing has slowed. Yawning is a reflex that brings more oxygen into the blood and moves more carbon dioxide out. This refreshes and replenishes the body, making us feel more awake.

Another theory says that yawning stretches the lungs. This helps to increase the heart rate and makes us feel less sluggish. A third theory says that yawning is a protective reflex that helps redistribute the oil-like substance called surfactant that helps lubricate the lungs on the inside and keeps them from collapsing.

How many facial expressions do humans have?

Scientists from Ohio State University in the USA have identified twenty-one facial expressions using a new computer software. Previously, scientists believed that people's faces expressed only six emotions—happy, sad, fearful, angry, surprised and disgusted. However, scientists have now tracked chemical pathways that control emotions in the brain. They believe that the brain is like a computer that reacts based on different combinations of inputs. As a result, it can produce twenty-one different emotions.

These twenty-one expressions are:

1. Happy
2. Sad
3. Fearful
4. Angry
5. Surprised
6. Disgusted
7. Happily surprised
8. Happily disgusted
9. Sadly fearful
10. Sadly angry
11. Awed
12. Disgustedly surprised
13. Angrily disgusted
14. Fearfully disgusted
15. Fearfully surprised
16. Angrily surprised
17. Sadly surprised
18. Sadly disgusted
19. Fearfully angry
20. Appalled
21. Hatred

What changes occur in my body when I sleep?

Many psychological and biological processes occur in the body when one is asleep. Sometimes while sleeping, the body jerks; the degree of the jerk is related to how tired one is, so the bigger the jerk, the more tired the body.

While we sleep, our body temperature reduces slightly in order to reduce the burning of calories. The body also goes through a toxin cleanse, which rejuvenates it and helps the brain to remove useless information. The brain makes important connections when the body rests and so it demands the most amount of oxygen when the body sleeps. The body's immune system also becomes hyperactive as tissues get repaired.

Why do we dream?

There are several theories as to why we dream. One states that dreams work hand in hand with sleep and help the brain scan and sort through all the information it has collected during the waking hours. This includes everything we see, feel and experience through the day. As the brain sorts through all this information, it keeps what's needed for future use and the rest is forgotten.

Why are dreams difficult to remember?

Dreams are normally stored in the frontal lobe of the cerebral cortex, which is the seat for short term memory. Usually, dreams can be recalled within the first five minutes of waking up. After that, they are forgotten. Most people have close to ten dreams a night and it is impossible to remember all of them. The only way a dream can be remembered is if one wakes up while dreaming or immediately after it.

What chemical reaction in the brain makes us dream when we sleep?

Scientists did not know much about the science of dreaming until 1953, when they learned about rapid eye movement (REM) and non-rapid eye movement (NREM), the two basic forms of sleep. Most of our dreams occur during REM sleep and three main chemicals are actively involved in this process.

The chemical acetylcholine is at its peak during REM sleep. This chemical is linked to memory formation and its high levels indicate that the brain is actively processing information during REM sleep. The level of another hormone, melatonin, is also particularly high during REM sleep. The brain releases more of this hormone when it is dark and it is responsible for making us feel sleepy. As a result, scientists believe we dream more deeply when melatonin levels are higher. A third hormone, called oxytocin, is also believed to play an important role in the process of dreaming. Also called the love hormone, oxytocin is associated with feelings of bonding and connectedness. Since we often dream of people we know and love, scientists believe oxytocin influences our dreams.

SENSATIONAL SENSES

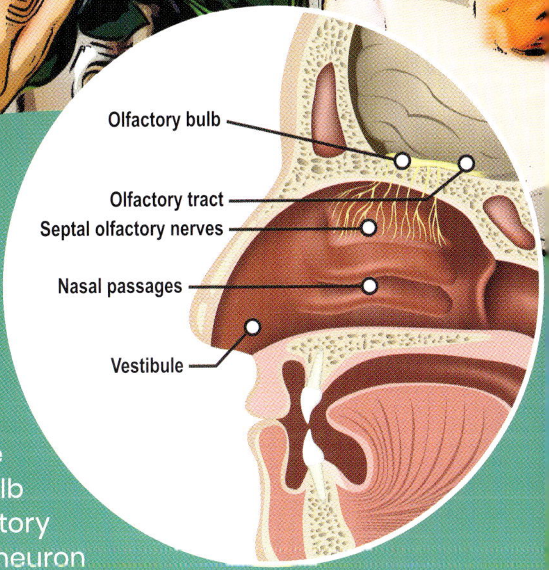

How do we smell?

At the back of the nose cavity, about 7 cm above and behind the nostrils, lies a special grouping of cells called the olfactory epithelium. These cells are attached to the olfactory bulb within the brain by olfactory neurons. At the end of each neuron lies a receptor cell. When something gives off a smell, tiny scent particles circulating in tho air attach to the receptor cells in the neurons and then send an electrical signal to the brain, which in turn senses the smell.

There are around 350 genes that actively control olfactory receptors in the human nose. Each gene produces a different type of receptor. Each specific receptor will react to a specific group of smells. A combination of several different receptors helps us sense different types of smells. Because our olfactory receptors are controlled by our genetic make-up, different people are sensitive to different types of scents. Some scientists believe humans can detect up to 1 trillion different scents!

Why do flowers make some people sneeze?

Many people sneeze when they come in contact with flowers. The main reason behind this is because flowers contain pollen. Pollen is a powdery substance that allows plants to reproduce. People who sneeze from being around pollen have an allergy to it. This allergy is also called hay fever and is caused because the person's body falsely believes that pollen will harm it. To prevent this harm, the body tries to get rid of the pollen from the nose and eyes through sneezing and producing tears. As a result, pollen allergies also cause itchy eyes and a runny nose. Pollen allergies generally occur seasonally, along with the seasonal cycles of plants that produce pollen.

What happens to my body when I sneeze?

When we sneeze, air from the lungs is expelled through the nose and mouth. Sneezing can be caused by an irritation to the nostrils, a fall in temperature, cold air or an infection. A sneeze begins with a tickling sensation in your nose, which sends a message to your brain that it needs to get rid of something that is irritating the area. Thus, a sneeze actually protects the body by clearing the nose of bacteria and foreign objects such as dust or insects. The nerves that send this message to the brain are not active while you are sleeping, so you cannot sneeze in your sleep.

Why does my mouth water on seeing food?

When we see food or think about it, our brain automatically signals the body to prepare for the process of digestion. Thus, on seeing food, the salivary glands start to secrete or give out saliva. Saliva, more commonly known as spit, is an enzyme that marks the start of digestion. During this stage, food combines with the saliva in the mouth and is broken down through biting into a mush called chyme. This chyme then proceeds further into the digestive tract to be processed, absorbed and excreted.

Why does the inside of my mouth feel cold after I eat mint candies?

Mint and peppermint contain a chemical compound called menthol. This compound activates the cold-sensitive receptors in the mouth. Once activated, these receptors start sending messages to the brain. The brain interprets these messages as a change in temperature, which leads to a cold sensation in the mouth, even though the actual temperature inside the mouth does not change. Peppermint has a higher concentration of menthol and so makes the mouth feel much cooler than mint.

What happens to my ears underwater?

The Eustachian tube in the ear works to ensure that the pressure inside and outside your ear remains the same. But when you are underwater, there is water on the outside of the eardrum and air on the inside. Water is denser than air because water molecules are more tightly packed together than air molecules. As a result, water exerts more pressure than air, which causes the pressure on the outside of the ear to be greater than the pressure on the inside. In order to balance out this difference, the eardrum stretches like a spring. Because the eardrum is full of nerves, this sort of stretching causes the eardrum to hurt.

Why do my ears pop or hurt when I go up a mountain or in an airplane?

The Eustachian tube that links the ear to the throat helps to maintain air pressure inside the ear. Its job is to ensure that the air pressure inside the ear is equal to the air pressure outside. This prevents us from feeling any discomfort when the air pressure around us changes.

When we travel to higher places—for example, in an elevator or airplane—the air pressure around us reduces. When this happens, the valve at the end of the Eustachian tube releases air to equalize the pressure inside the ear. This results in the sensation of our ears popping.

Popping can wear off with actions like swallowing or yawning. However, when the ears don't pop, you may feel pain as air pushes against the eardrums. Sometimes it takes a few days after returning to lower ground for the ears to pop, but if this doesn't happen, a visit to the doctor may be needed.

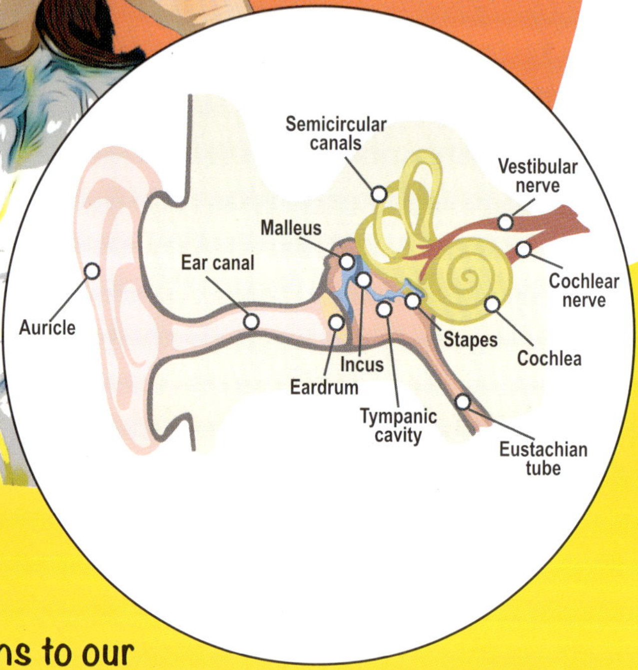

What happens to our sense of hearing when we listen to loud music?

Sound waves pass from the outer ear to the inner ear through the middle ear. As a sound wave travels through the ear, it sets off a series of reactions. The eardrum vibrates in the middle ear and the tiny hair cells present in the inner ear transmit a chemical signal to the brain, which is then interpreted as sound.

When our ears are overexposed to loud music, the hair cells in the inner ear get overworked and this causes disturbances in the signals that are transmitted to the brain. And so, the brain fails to interpret the sound. The louder the sound, the more the pressure on the inner ear, which causes more damage to the hair cells. Once affected, hair cells cannot be replaced and this can lead to permanent loss of hearing!

How does the human eye work?

Though the eyes provide vision in all animals, the human eye works differently as compared to the eyes of other creatures. The human eye responds to light and pressure, which allows it to see a three-dimensional moving image. The human eye can also differentiate between about ten million colours.

When the human eye is able to see an object, it is actually receiving light signals. This changes the size of the pupil or that part of the eye which controls how much light enters it. The eyes collect light from the surroundings and focus it to form an image. Once the image is formed, it is converted into electrical impulses or signals that are sent to the brain. When the brain reads the signals, we are able to perceive or see things.

What is the resolution of the human eye?

In microscopes, televisions and cameras, resolution is usually measured in pixels. The strength of the human eye, however, is measured by the number of line pairs it can see in a defined space. This is expressed in degrees and is called the eyes' spatial acuity.

The centre of the eye, called the fovea, is where the eye captures the best image. It is also interesting to note that the size of the human eye's pupil changes throughout the day in order to view things at different distances. For example, during the day, the pupil size ranges between 3 and 4 mm and increases to between 5 and 9 mm at night.

Taking all this into consideration, scientists have been able to approximate the resolution of the human eye in pixels and found it to be 576 megapixels for full 360-degree viewing. However, humans don't actually have 360-degree vision. A more realistic measure, based on looking at something that is about twenty-four inches away, is about 300 pixels per inch.

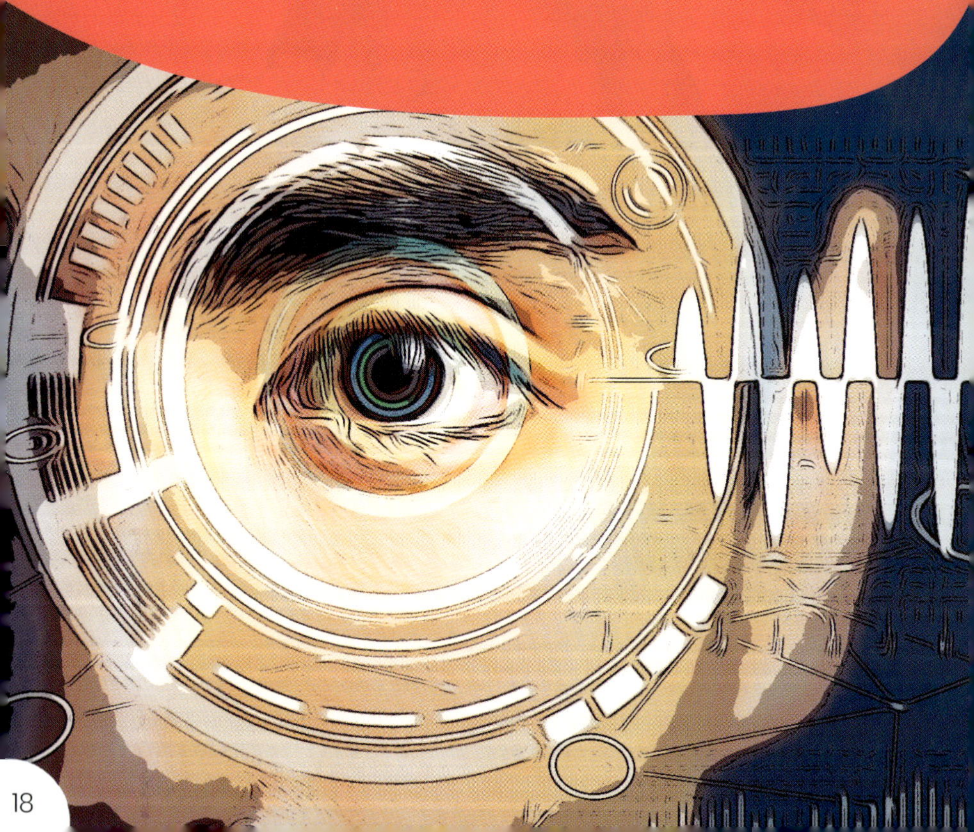

Why do I blink my eyes?

Blinking is the quick closing and opening of eyelids. It takes around 400 milliseconds for our eyes to blink once! Although the speed of blinking is affected by various conditions like tiredness, use of medication and certain health issues, changes in the speed of blinking often go unnoticed.

Our eyes mainly blink to clear dust particles and provide moisture to the eyeballs. The eyeballs receive moisture from a tear film, which is made of water, oil, mucus and various nutrients and natural antibiotics that keep the eyes healthy. When we blink, glands in the body secrete the components of the tear film to renew it. Scientists have also found that eyes blink to get a moment of rest so that they can focus better.

Why do people from different parts of the world have different coloured eyes?

The coloured part of the human eye is called the iris. The colour of the iris is related to the amount of melanin it contains. Melanin is a coloured substance in our body that also determines the colour of our skin and hair. Eye colour is hereditary, which means that we are likely to have the same eye colour as our parents or siblings.

Sixteen different genes are associated with the colour of the eye. Human eyes have nine broad categories of colour. Of these, the gene for brown eyes is the strongest and the gene for blue eyes the weakest. The colour hazel lies between the lightest blue and the darkest brown eyes. It is believed that only two per cent of the world has green-coloured eyes and all people with blue-coloured eyes have one common ancestor. Eye colour can also change dramatically in the first few years of life. In fact, many babies are born with blue eyes but later develop green or brown eyes.

What is heterochromia?

Heterochromia is a condition in which the two irises of a living being are of different colours. Heterochromia can be seen in humans and other species such as cats and dogs, and can be of different types. Complete heterochromia refers to the condition where one iris is of a different colour than the other. Partial heterochromia refers to the condition where only a part of one iris is of a different colour than the rest. Central heterochromia refers to the condition where the inner circle of the iris is differently coloured from the outer area.

This condition could arise due to many reasons. When one is born with it, it is known as congenital heterochromia. According to studies, for most infants born with heterochromia, the condition is hereditary and they do not have any other problems with their eyes or their health. However, some infants are born with heterochromia because of a disease called Horner's syndrome. It includes a combination of symptoms that arise when a group of nerves known as the sympathetic trunk is damaged. A person can be affected by heterochromia later on in life too; this is called acquired heterochromia. It can be caused due to an eye injury, eye surgery, bleeding in the eye or acquired Horner's syndrome.

Why do my eyes water while cutting onions?

When you cut an onion, you are cutting into its cells. This releases a compound called sulphenic acid, which further breaks down into a gas called syn-propanethial S-oxide. When this gas mixes with the water in your eyes, it produces small amounts of sulphuric acid which irritates the nose and eyes. As an automatic response, your eyes blink and produce tears. The tears produced wash out the acid, which could otherwise damage the eyes. One way to prevent your eyes from watering while cutting onions is to place the onions in water before you start cutting them.

What happens to my eyes when I wear contact lenses for a long time?

Contact lenses sit on the clear protective layer of the eyes known as the cornea. When you wear contact lenses, your corneas are covered entirely, and this prevents them from receiving oxygen. Oxygen is necessary to keep the eyes healthy and wearing contact lenses for too long can damage the cornea. Nowadays, contact lenses are made using materials that allow oxygen to reach the cornea through the lens.

Long term use of contact lenses can also dry out the eyes. What's more, using old lenses or those that are past their expiration date can damage our eyes. Germs and bacteria accumulate on the pores of such old lenses and can give us eye infections.

What happens to human eyes in the dark?

Even though the human eye is capable of some amazing things, it cannot give us perfect night vision that many animals, especially animals that hunt, have. Human beings can see in the dark, but it takes the eyes approximately twenty to thirty minutes to adjust to complete darkness. During this time, the sensitivity of our eyes increases by one million times. This happens because of the expansion of our pupils, the part of the eye that controls how much light gets in. Our eye's ability to see colour also changes in the dark. Young people are better at adapting to seeing in the dark as compared to the elderly.

What happens to my eyes when I am asleep and dreaming?

Even when you are asleep, your eyes are still functioning. However, they can only sense light versus dark, which is why a bright light or the sunrise can often wake you up.

Your eyes go through two different sleep stages. When you go to sleep, you don't enter the dream state immediately. But once you do, your eyeballs start moving from side to side, almost like they would when you are awake and looking at things. This stage is known as rapid eye movement or REM, and the tiny eye movements are known as saccades. Saccades are said to be the fastest movements produced by the human body. It is during this stage that we see dreams and according to researchers, every time an eye movement is registered, the brain also shows a spark of activity.

Non-REM sleep is the stage when the eyes are motionless and the body is relaxed. During this time, brainwaves and blood pressure are slower than normal. The eyes don't send any information to the brain, and the connection between the eyes and the brain reboots only when you wake up.

How much hair does a person have on their head?

Most humans have close to 1,00,000 hairs on their scalp that grow at the rate of six inches a year. However, this number and rate can vary due to various factors like pollution, medication, ailments and personal care routines. While large amounts of hair are usually seen only on the head, the entire surface of the human body has about 50,00,000 hairs!

Some years ago, a German scientist counted the number of hairs on the heads of different people. He found that they vary in number, depending upon the colour of the hair. A black-haired person will have a lot more hair than a red-haired person, a brown-haired person will have thicker hair than a black-haired person and a blonde will have the densest hair as compared to the rest.

Is hair a non-living thing?

A single hair strand has two main parts—the visible part known as the shaft and the invisible root, also known as the hair follicle or hair bulb. The shaft is made of keratin. Keratin is a type of protein that is found in our cells. This keratin is also found in animal horns and wool as well as bird feathers.

Keratinized protein cells are produced by the living hair bulb, which is found at the bottom of each hair strand. As these cells move away from the hair bulb, which is the growing region of the hair, they die. Thus, the visible hair is dead whereas the hair follicle or bulb, which is located in the layer of the skin called the epidermis, is living.

What happens to my hair when I oil it?

Oil coats the hair shaft to form a protective layer. This helps protect the hair from all kinds of damage while the vital nutrients in the oil nourish the hair. Oil increases the strength of the hair, reduces frizz and prevents breakage. If the oil is applied using a soft massaging technique, it stimulates the circulation of blood to the scalp, which acts as a stress-buster and reduces hair fall.

However, when you leave oil on the roots of the hair for too long, it blocks the pores and doesn't allow oxygen to reach the roots, and causes hair loss. It's best to massage the head with warm oil and leave it in for an hour before washing it off with shampoo.

Why do our eyebrows and eyelashes not grow very long?

The hair follicles on our eyebrows and eyelashes are just like the ones on our arms and legs. However, they are different from the follicles on the scalp. Scalp follicles produce hair from the excessive proteins present in the body at a continuous rate. As a result, hair on the head can grow very long. The other hair follicles present in the body, including those on our eyebrows and eyelashes, go through growth cycles. This means that the hair grows for a certain period of time, after which it stops growing and falls out. This cycle keeps repeating and as a result, the hair doesn't grow very long. What's more, even if you pull out the hair on your eyebrows and eyelashes—and they will come out easily—they will grow back again in no time!

Why does the skin tan?

Ultraviolet (UV) radiation from sunlight can damage human skin. When UV rays penetrate right up to the lower layers of the skin, they trigger cells called melanocytes that produce melanin—the brown pigment that causes tanning. These melanocytes move closer to the skin's surface and produce more melanin, which further browns or darkens the skin, creating a suntan.

The role of the melanin is to absorb UV radiation and defend the skin from damage. A skin tan is thus the body's way of protecting itself from harmful UV rays that can damage cells and cause ailments like skin cancer.

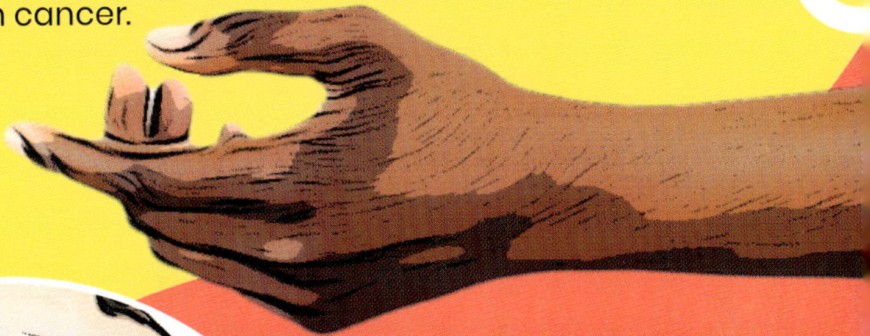

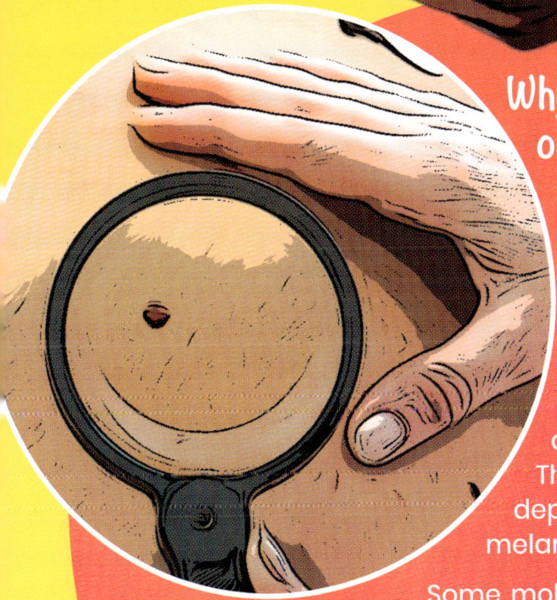

Why do I have moles on my body?

Moles are small bumps or areas of changed skin colour that occur on any part of the skin. Most moles are brownish in colour, but they can be flesh coloured, blue or black. The colour of the mole depends on the amount of melanin at that spot.

Some moles are present at birth, while others appear during the first twenty years of life, especially during puberty. Moles are caused by the overproduction of melanin. At first, moles appear flat, but they may grow larger and develop hair. If you have a mole that changes colour or size, you need to let your doctor know about it.

What is acne?

Acne is a skin condition that usually shows up when you enter your teenage years. Acne can occur in many forms—whiteheads, blackheads, red bumps called pimples and bumps that are filled with pus called pustules. Most acne is formed due to the clogging of the pores on the face, back or chest.

Your skin is covered with tiny holes called pores that contain oil glands, also known as sebaceous glands. Most of the time, these glands secrete the right amount of sebum or oil and the pores are fine. But sometimes, the pores get clogged up with too much sebum, dead skin cells and germs. This results in the formation of acne.

What is a birthmark?

A coloured mark on or under a newborn baby's skin is known as a birthmark. These marks usually show up as soon as a baby is born. Some birthmarks fade or disappear as a child gets older while others stay or sometimes get bigger, darker or even thicker.

Birthmarks are formed from extra melanin in the skin or from blood vessels that are bunched together or have grown abnormally. Most birthmarks are harmless and do not cause pain. However, if there is any kind of change in the shape or colour of a birthmark, it should be brought to the attention of a doctor immediately.

What happens to my skin when I rub it with lemon?

Lemons have antifungal and antibacterial properties which kill bacteria that produce acne. Lemons are also natural exfoliators—the citric acid in a lemon can remove dead skin to an extent. Lemon juice acts as an astringent and closes the skin's pores, which makes it smooth to touch. Lemon juice is also acidic in nature and acts as a natural bleach. However, one shouldn't apply lemon juice on the skin when it is exposed to sunlight as this can cause damage. Those with dry skin should not apply lemon juice directly onto the skin as this could make the skin drier.

What happens to my skin when I get burnt?

When one gets burnt, it starts off a chain of reactions within the body. The immune system sends platelets and repair cells to the affected area, which causes redness and swelling. This response helps to heal the cells at the site of the burn and also stops foreign particles or bacteria from irritating the area further.

First-degree burns are those that affect only the skin and cause redness, swelling and pain. Such burns can most often be treated at home. Second-degree burns are more serious because they affect underlying tissue and cause blisters too. In extreme third-degree burns, when the burn has gone through the skin, often down to the bone, the burnt region swells up, causing infection. In extreme cases, the body may also go into shock.

How do fingernails grow?

Our nails are made up of three parts—the matrix, the cuticle and the lunula. Each nail begins growing at the matrix or root, in a little pocket under the skin. The matrix is constantly making new cells and these new cells keep pushing the older cells up through the skin to form the nail. By the time the cells emerge from under the skin, they are dead.

The cuticle is the thin piece of skin from where the nail grows out of your finger. It protects the matrix. Sometimes, the nail has a whitish half-moon like shape at the base, which is known as the lunula.

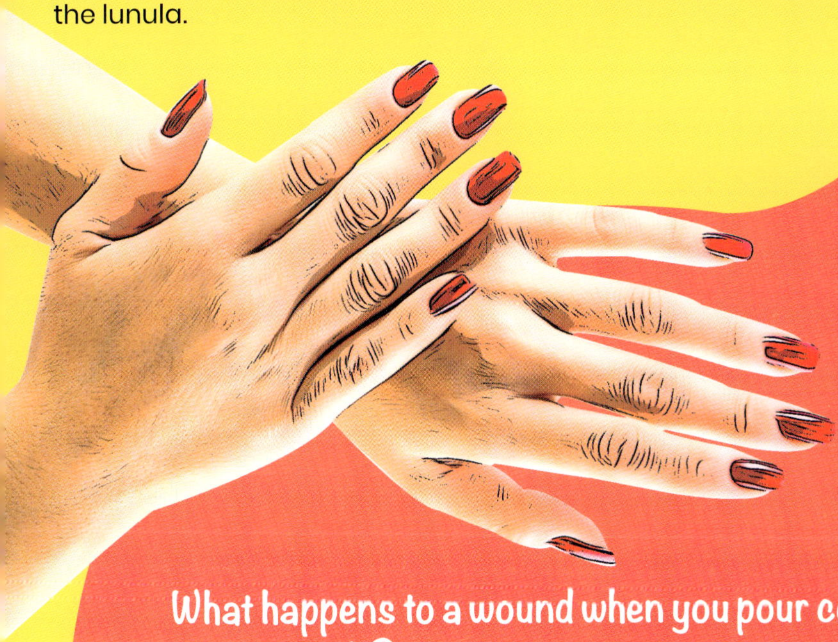

What happens to a wound when you pour cold water over it?

Water removes dirt and bacteria from a wound. When you have a wound that is bleeding, cold water will make the blood vessels contract, which will slow down the flow of blood and stop the bleeding. Cold water is ideal because hot water can burn the tissue around the wound and ice can increase tissue damage. Minor burns can also be soothed with cold water. However, if there is a lot of dirt stuck on a wound, it should be washed with lukewarm water as this will help loosen the dirt and clean the wound better.

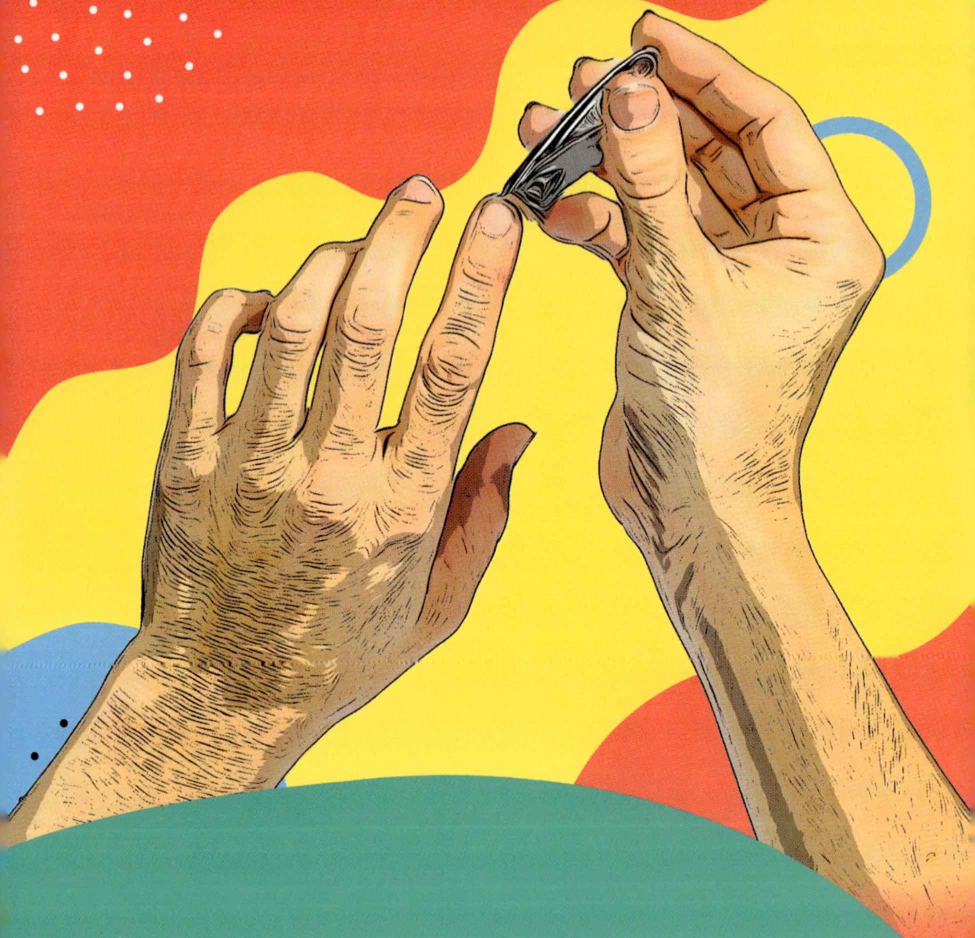

Why does cutting fingernails not hurt?

Fingernails are formed from dead cells. They have no blood supply or nerve supply and therefore cannot feel any pain. However, if one hurts the skin under a fingernail, or cuts the skin under a fingernail, it would hurt and could also bleed.

Similarly, if one was to drop a heavy object on their fingernail or get their fingernail caught in a door, they are sure to feel a lot of pain! This is because the force from the blow goes well past the nail, to the finger underneath, which is full of sensory nerves. And so, there is pain. The nail may also turn blue because of a blood clot underneath and could sting for a few days.

THE HEALTHY HEART

How does the heart function?

The heart is a muscular organ and is usually the size of a person's fist. It is responsible for pumping blood all across the body through veins, arteries and capillaries. The human heart is divided into four chambers—two upper chambers or atria and two lower chambers or ventricles.

The right atrium receives impure or de-oxygenated blood from everywhere in the body. This blood is then pumped into the right ventricle from where it is sent to the lungs to get oxygenated. The blood from the lungs is further sent to the left atrium, from where it is pumped to the left ventricle, which is the strongest chamber of the heart. From here, the blood is pumped back to all parts of the body. The oxygen in this pumped blood is used by the body's cells to produce energy. The left ventricle's contractions are measured as blood pressure.

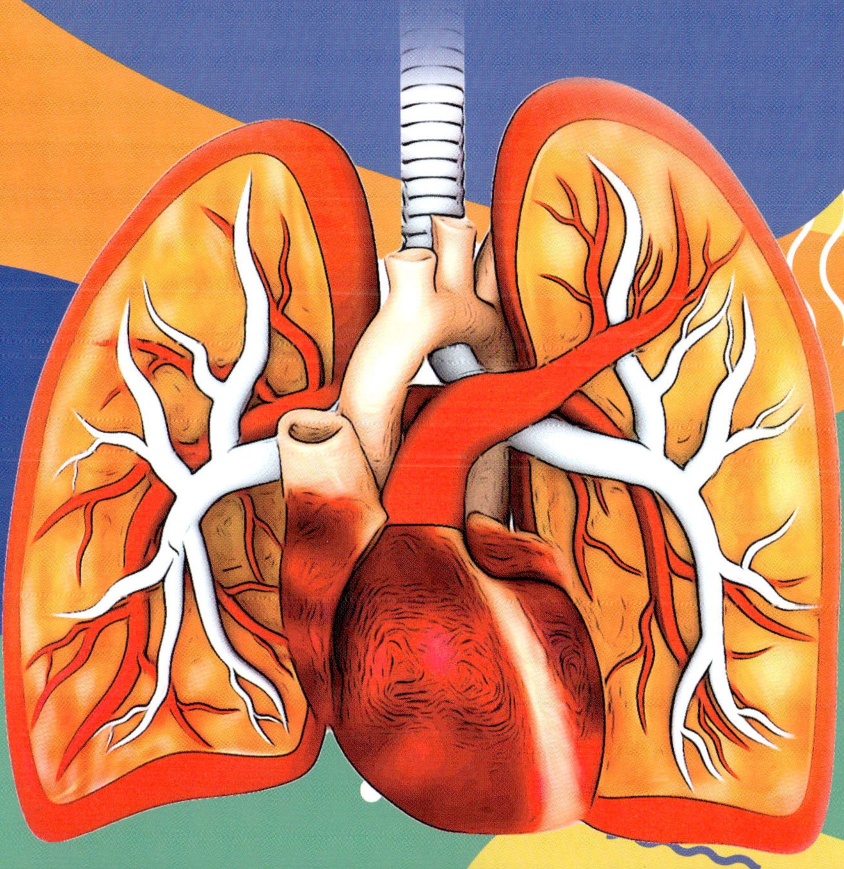

How big is the human heart?

The human heart measures about 12 cm in length, 8 cm in width and 6 cm in thickness. It is the size of a closed fist and weighs about 300 gm in men and slightly less in women.

The heart weighs approximately 0.5 per cent of the total body weight. However, the heart grows to match the amount of work it has to do. A foetal heart, or the heart of an unborn baby, is very different from that of a baby and an adult.

Different species of animals have different-sized hearts. For instance, the blue whale has the largest heart that weighs close to 180 kg whereas the smallest heart belongs to a type of fruit fly and is only 0.21 mm in length.

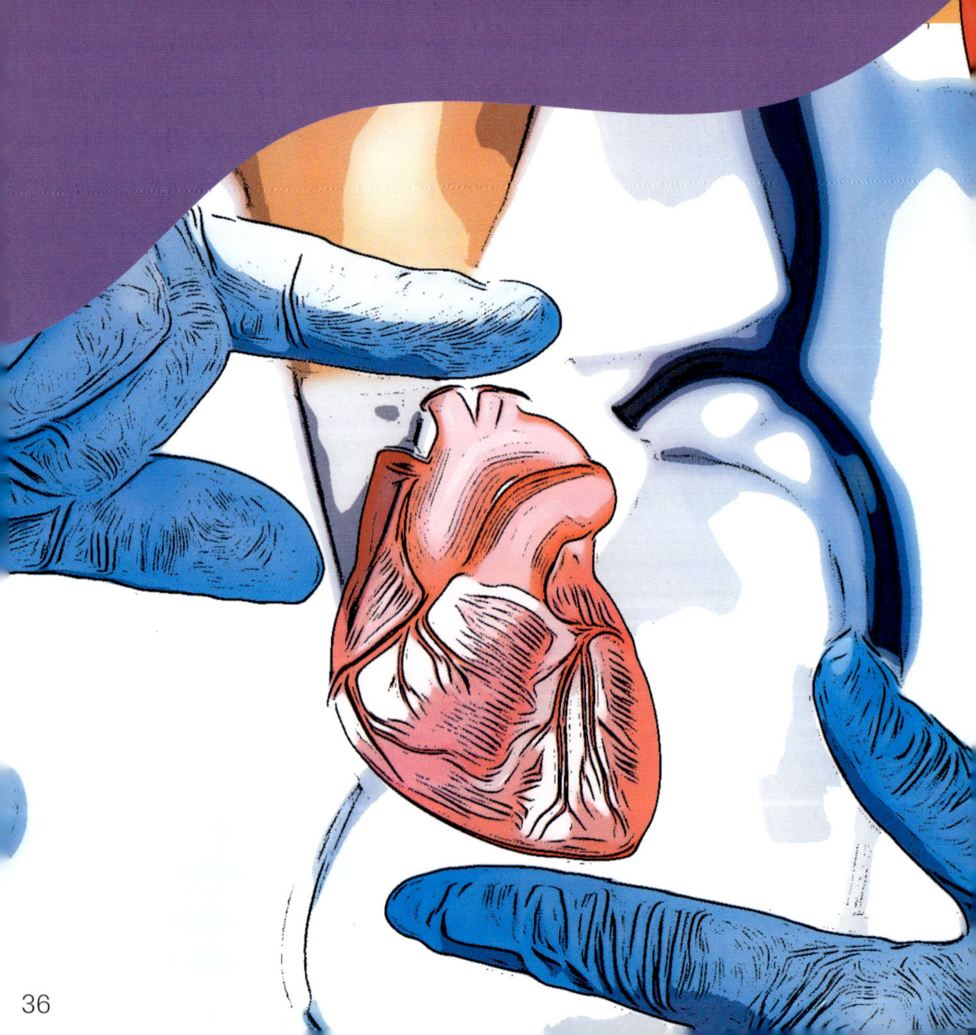

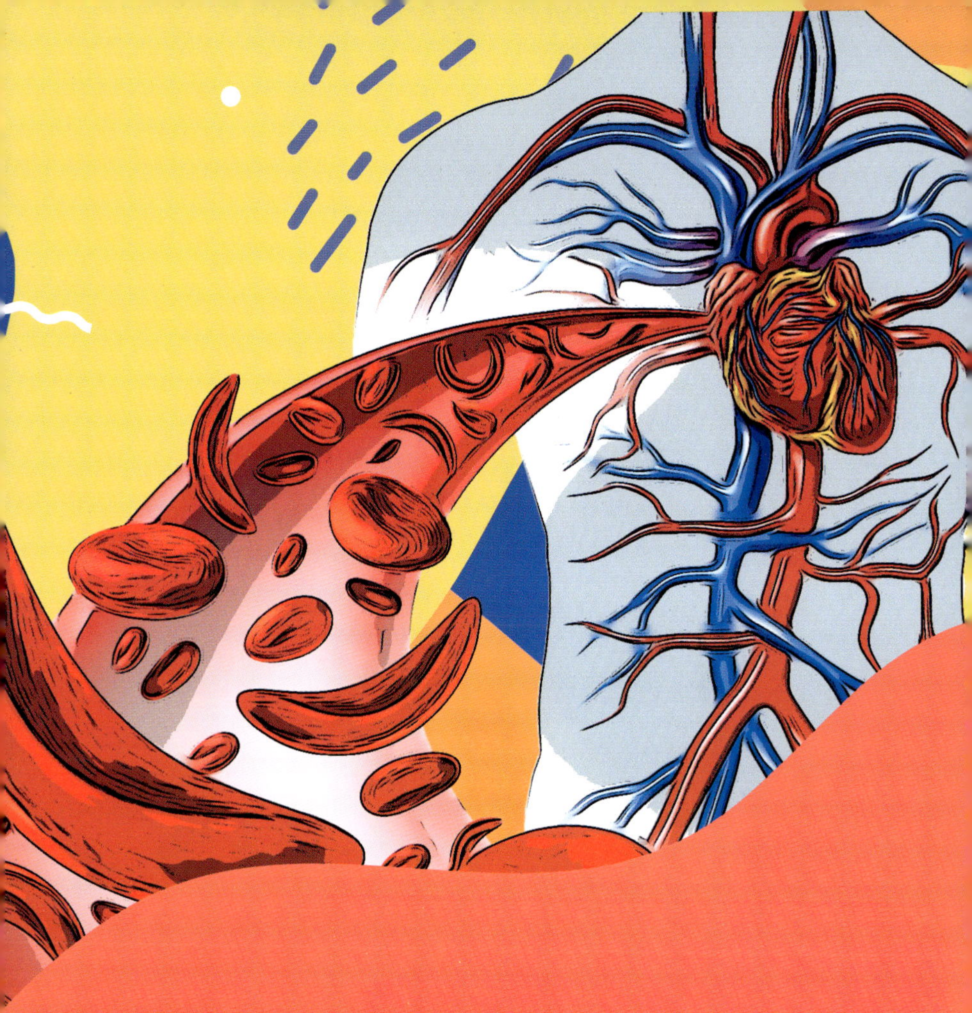

How much blood does the human heart pump?

The human body has close to five litres of blood that circulates through the heart to various parts of the body approximately every forty-five seconds. To enable this flow, the heart beats about 1,00,000 times in twenty-four hours. While an adult's heart beats at an average of seventy-two times a minute, a new-born baby's heart beats much faster—between eighty and 190 times a minute.

Each time the heart beats, sixty to ninety millilitres of blood is pumped out of the heart for it to reach different parts of the body. The heart pumps out oxygenated blood, which flows through the arteries. The blood coming back to the heart is deoxygenated blood, which flows from various body parts through the veins.

What happens during a heart attack?

Most heart attacks are caused when there is excessive fat deposited within the blood vessels that supply blood to the heart. This deposition reduces the space available within the vessels for blood to flow. As a result, less amount of oxygenated blood reaches the heart, causing pain and discomfort. Sometimes these fatty deposits, known as plaque, become dislodged and flow towards the heart, causing a blockage that completely cuts off the blood supply to the heart. This leads to a cardiac arrest or heart attack. Most men feel a lot of pain and discomfort when they get a heart attack while women can also feel nauseous and short of breath.

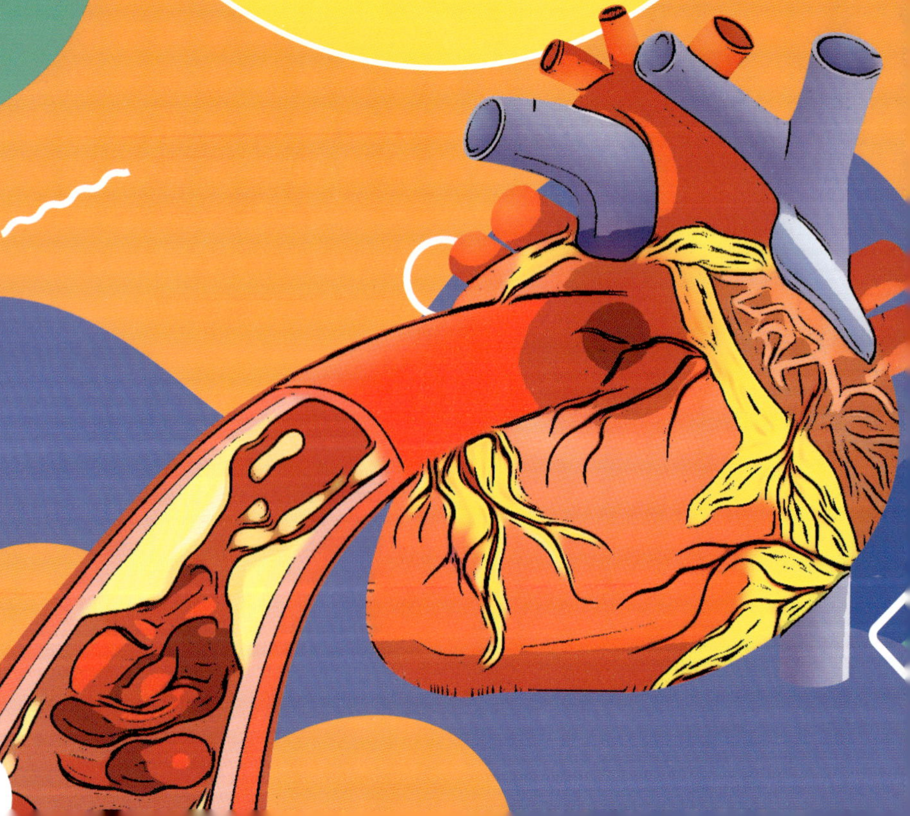

How does a doctor examine a patient's pulse and why?

Pulse is the rhythmic throbbing that can be felt as blood flows through your arteries. It is a measure of the rate at which your heart beats. It can be felt on the human body in places such as the wrist and neck, though doctors usually check it at the wrist. While checking the pulse, the doctor places their finger on the artery in the wrist and counts how many times a throbbing is felt in one minute.

Doctors measure the pulse to know how healthy a patient's heart is and if blood is being pumped properly across the body. The normal resting heart rate for adults is between 60 and 100 beats per minute. If the patient is in any kind of shock, the pulse may be lower than normal. If the patient suffers from heart issues or high blood pressure, the pulse may be higher than normal.

Why do some babies have a hole in their heart?

A hole in the heart is a genetic defect. All babies have a hole between the two upper chambers of the heart when they are in their mother's womb. This hole usually closes up before birth. But in some cases, the hole, which is closed by a natural flap, doesn't seal before birth. Babies with this condition are called blue babies.

In some cases, the hole may seal in a week or a few months after the baby is born. But in some cases, the hole doesn't heal at all. This defect changes the normal flow of blood through the heart and needs to be corrected with the help of a doctor.

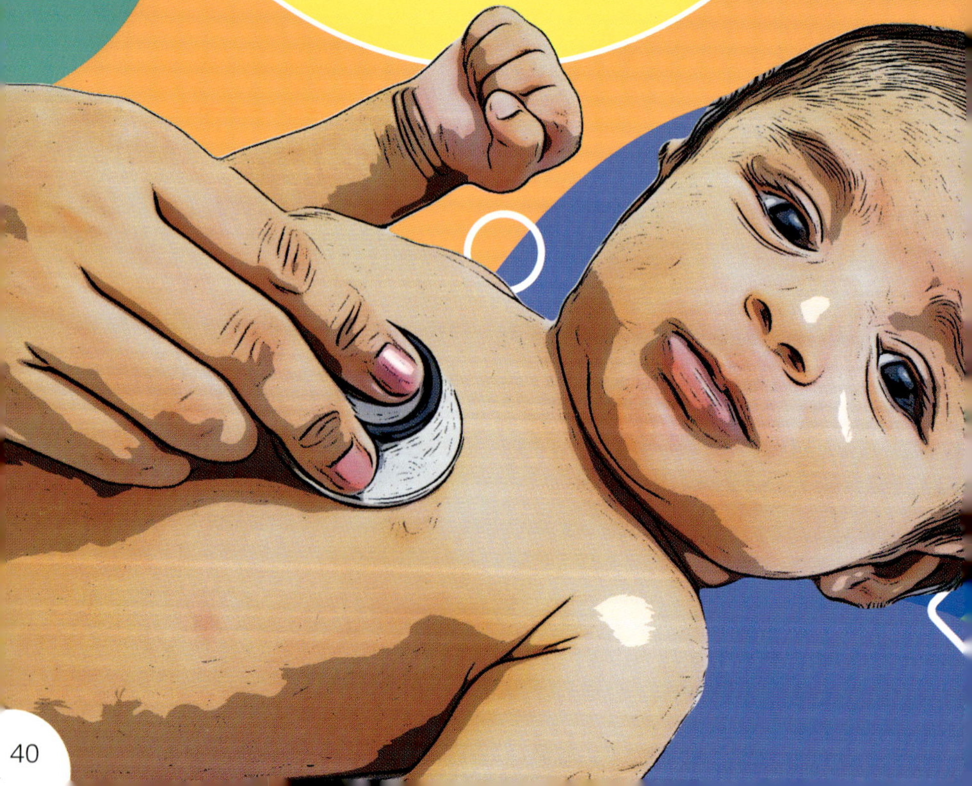

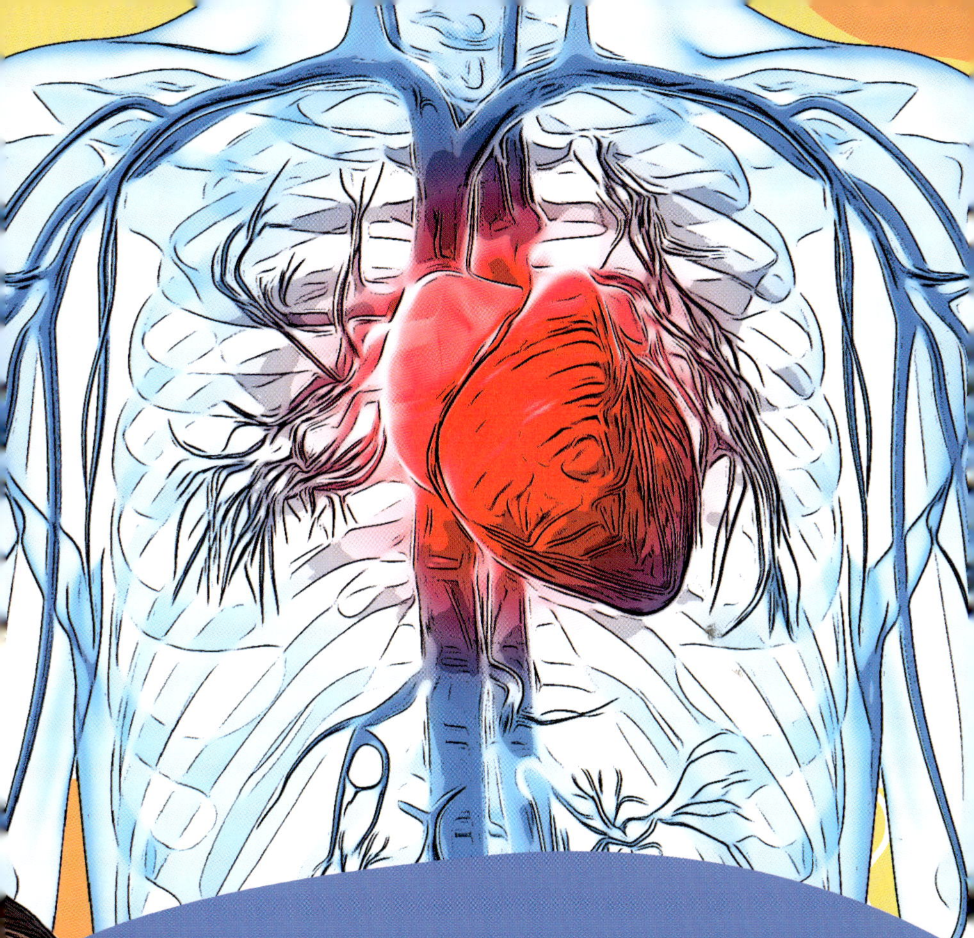

What happens if a person's heart is on the right side instead of left?

The heart is located in the chest cavity, which is almost in the centre of the body, but about two-thirds of the heart is towards the left and one-third is towards the right. It is placed safely behind the sternum or breastbone, between the lungs and above the diaphragm.

Sometimes, when a baby is still in the mother's womb, its heart develops towards the right side of the chest, instead of the normal left side. This condition is known as dextrocardia. Though the condition is not serious and people can live with it, it can lead to changes in the placement of some digestive organs, which in turn can affect the lifespan of a person with this condition.

How are heart transplants conducted?

In a heart transplant, a surgeon removes the faulty heart and places a new heart in its place. When a new heart is placed, the arteries and veins need to be reconnected to it so that oxygen rich blood can flow away from the heart and oxygen-lacking blood can flow to it.

A heart transplant is done only in those cases where medicines and other surgeries have failed and there is no other scope of treatment. The first successful human-to-human heart transplant was conducted in 1967 by Dr. Christiaan Barnard. Today, scientists are working towards making it possible to conduct human heart transplants using the heart of a pig!

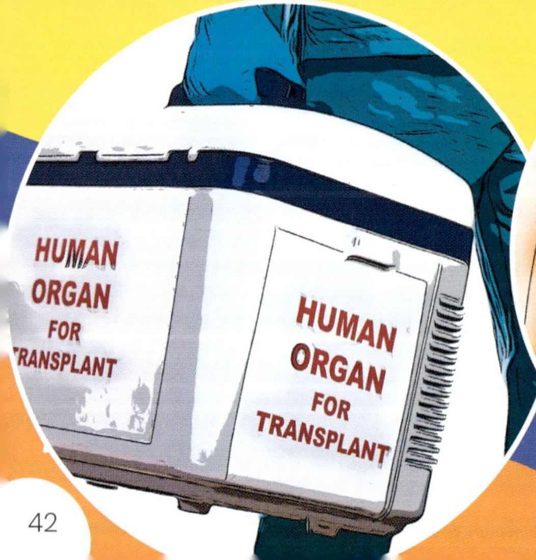

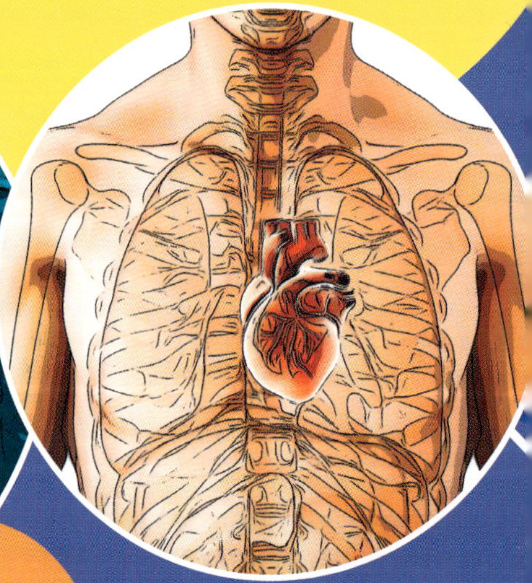

DIGEST THIS!

How long does food remain in the digestive system?

The time food takes to travel from the mouth to the rectum differs from person to person and also according to the food that has been eaten. In most cases, food takes six to eight hours to pass through the stomach and enter your large intestine, where further digestion and absorption of water occurs before the undigested food is finally eliminated out of the body through the rectum.

The time food spends in the intestine varies from thirty-six hours to as long as five days, before exiting the body. Fruits and vegetables get digested fastest. Protein-rich foods like meat take longer and red meat takes the longest.

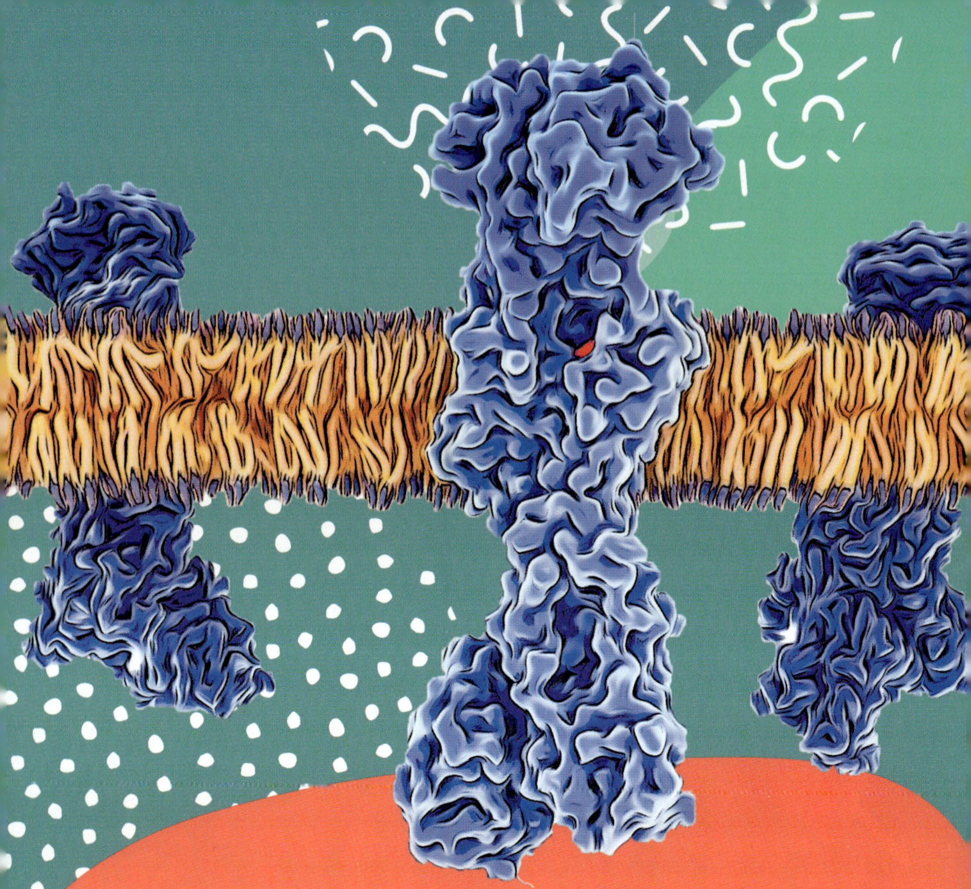

What are the different enzymes the body uses during digestion?

Enzymes are essential for the healthy functioning of the body. They work with other chemicals in the body, such as bile and stomach acid, to break down the food we eat into substances that the body is able to absorb. Some enzymes also bind substances present in the food we eat together to produce chemical compounds that can be absorbed or used by the body.

During digestion, the body uses three specific kinds of enzymes. These are proteases that break down protein into amino acids; lipases that break down fat into fatty acids and glycerol; and amylases that break down starches and carbohydrates into simple sugars. These amino acids, fatty acids, carbohydrates and simple sugars are easier for the body to absorb and use for energy production and various essential functions.

How does exercise help improve digestion?

Certain kinds of exercises are good for the digestive system as they help reduce problems like flatulence (gassiness) and acidity. Walking is an especially good exercise to help clear out waste material from the digestive system. A raised heart rate, which follows exercise, also makes the intestines function more efficiently, thus improving digestion.

Yoga is another form of exercise that helps with digestion and clearing waste from the body. In certain yoga asanas or poses, the liver is twisted. This twisting squeezes the liver and detoxifies it. Aerobic exercises that improve breathing also bring more enzymes to the digestive system, thus helping in the digestion of food.

What makes my stomach growl?

Stomach noises such as rumbling and gurgling are typically caused during the process of digestion. The growling can occur before a meal when you are hungry, or during or after a meal, when the food is being digested.

Hunger and appetite are controlled by a complex system. When one hasn't eaten for a while, the stomach sends a message to the brain, which produces a desire to eat. Simultaneously, a message is sent to the stomach and intestines. This triggers contractions in the stomach muscles and releases acids and other digestive fluids that prepare the body for the food a person will eat. This is what causes the rumbling sounds in the stomach. Interestingly, just the thought, smell or sight of food can cause the stomach to rumble too.

What happens to my body if I hold in a fart?

The gases in your gut are a mix of oxygen, carbon dioxide, nitrogen, hydrogen, methane and small amounts of hydrogen sulphide. Some of these gases, like oxygen, hydrogen and methane, can be absorbed by the gut, but nitrogen finds its way out of the body as a fart.

The longer the gas is held inside the body, the stronger and smellier it gets. What's more, some of the gas may also come out through the mouth in the form of a burp or create bubbles in your intestines, which can be painful.

What happens to my body when I overeat?

Very often, people lose track of the amount of food they have consumed, especially when they eat too fast. The size of a person's stomach is equal to the size of their closed fist. But as the stomach is a muscular sac, it can expand up to three times its original size depending on the amount of food you put in it.

On average, the stomach can hold three litres of food or fluid. When the amount of food consumed is more than the stomach's capacity to expand, it can cause nausea, heartburn and discomfort.

What causes diarrhoea and an upset stomach?

Diarrhoea is nothing but watery stools. It can occur when a person is allergic to specific foods like milk or prawns, or one has consumed spoilt food, or one has an infection in the stomach or intestines. Sometimes, certain medicines can also cause diarrhoea.

Diarrhoea can serve as a quick way for the body to rid itself of toxins or bacteria. However, it can lead to the loss of bodily fluids like water as well as essential salts in the body. This can be harmful, especially for young children and those with heart ailments. It is therefore advised to drink lots of water when one is suffering from diarrhoea.

What happens to chewing gum that is swallowed?

Chewing gum cannot be broken down in the stomach or the digestive system like other foods can. It simply moves through the digestive system and gets eliminated out of the body along with other wastes. However, sometimes, a large piece of chewing gum could get stuck in the stomach or other parts of the digestive system and create a blockage in the digestive tract. These blockages are most likely when chewing gum is swallowed along with other non-digestible materials or objects like un-soaked sunflower seeds or melon seeds.

Why do I get hiccups?

Hiccups are uncontrollable muscle movements or spasms of the diaphragm, a muscle in our abdomen. In most cases, hiccups are caused by eating or drinking something too quickly. Hiccups can also be caused by a food item that has irritated the stomach and caused it to become bloated. The stomach lies below the diaphragm and when it bloats, it makes the diaphragm contract at quick intervals, leading to hiccups.

There are many ways to stop hiccups. Sometimes, taking a deep breath or holding one's breath works; breathing into a paper bag can also do the trick. Scientifically speaking, as soon as the amount of carbon dioxide in the lungs increases, it relaxes the diaphragm and thus halts the spasms.

How do heavy metals enter the human body?

Heavy metals include elements like lead, mercury and cadmium. These metals occur naturally and are found in rocks and soil. The natural breakdown of rocks and soil releases heavy metals into seas, rivers and lakes, which then settle on the floor of the water bodies. Heavy metals also enter water bodies because of industrial pollution.

When plants grow on the floor of a water body, they absorb the heavy metals along with other nutrients. When fish feed on these plants, the heavy metals automatically pass on to these animals. Sadly, heavy metals do not break down, and so repeated intake of heavy metal-laden foods causes a build-up of heavy metals in aquatic creatures.

Some heavy metals become more concentrated when larger animals eat smaller animals for food as part of the food chain. This is called biomagnification. When humans consume these larger animals as food, they are consuming the heavy metals too. These heavy metals get lodged in human beings' internal organs, causing various ailments and in extreme cases, poisoning.

What role does the liver play in digestion?

The liver is responsible for the production of bile. Bile is secreted into the small intestine, where it helps digest certain vitamins and fat The liver also plays an important role in removing chemicals and toxins such as ammonia from our body that could otherwise cause damage. Another important function of the liver is the removal of sugar from blood. The liver stores sugar as glycogen, which the body converts to glucose when it needs to generate energy. Thus, the liver is responsible for breaking down fats, storing energy and releasing nutrients for the body to use as and when required.

What are good and bad bacteria and how do they help with digestion?

Many bacterial forms exist in the body—while certain useful or good bacteria help with digestion, other bacteria can cause ailments. One of the most important forms of good bacteria is lactobacteria, which are found in the small intestine. These bacteria help digest milk products and break down the sugar lactose that is found in them.

Bifidobacteria are another type of good bacteria that live in the colon. These bacteria produce vitamin B, help with bowel movements and produce antibiotics that kill bad bacteria. Bacteria like E. Coli or staphylococcus are bad bacteria that create trouble by causing infections of the skin and the gut.

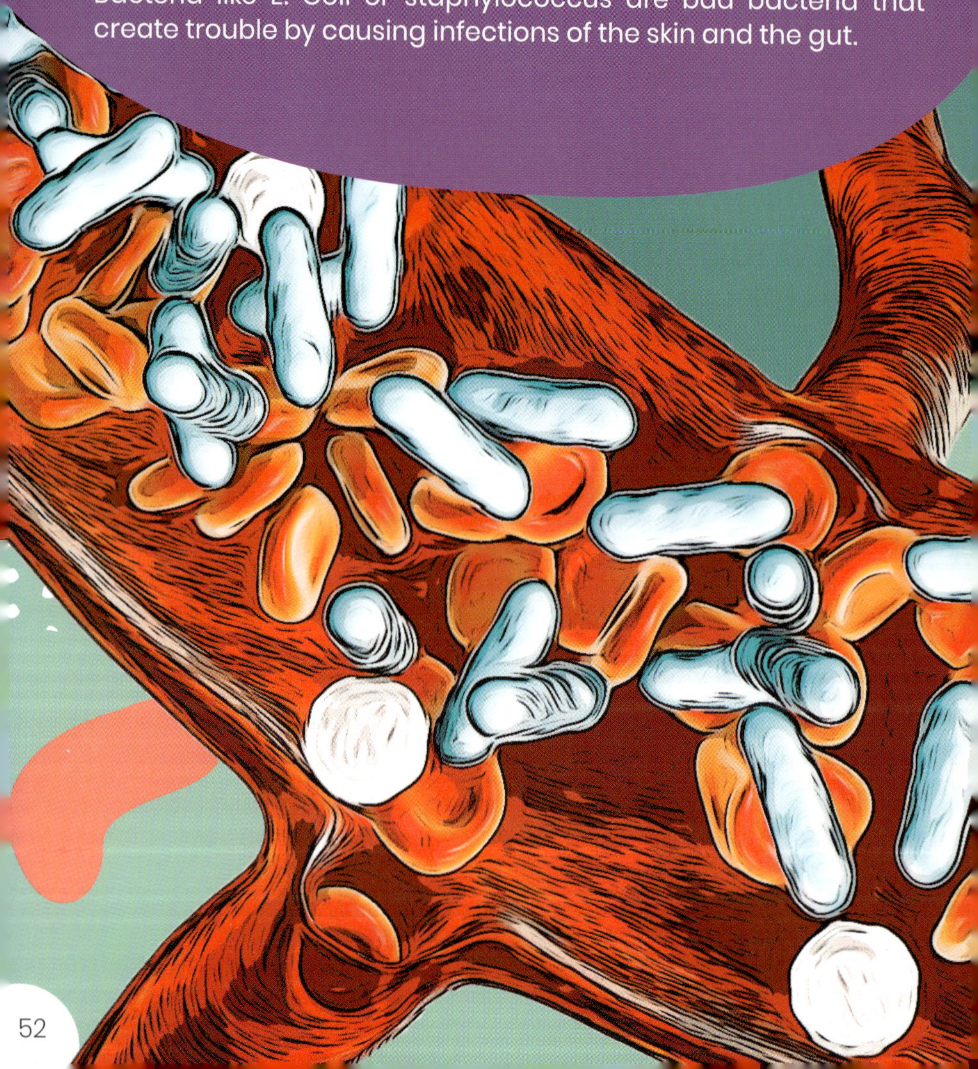

STRONG BONES, MIGHTY MUSCLES!

What are the different kinds of bones in the human body?

The human body has five different types of bones—sesamoid, irregular, flat, long and short. Each type of bone is equipped for a different function.

Sesamoid bones include those that are found in the hands, knees and feet. These bones protect the tendons from damage and wear and tear, for example the kneecap. Irregular bones have different shapes—some could be long whereas others could be curved. Their main function is to protect organs, for example the bones of the spinal cord.

Flat bones are shield-like and are often seen with muscles attached to them, like the pelvic bones. Long bones support weight and movement and are seen in the arms and legs. Short bones are always cuboid in shape, for example the bones in our wrists. They help with movement and provide stability.

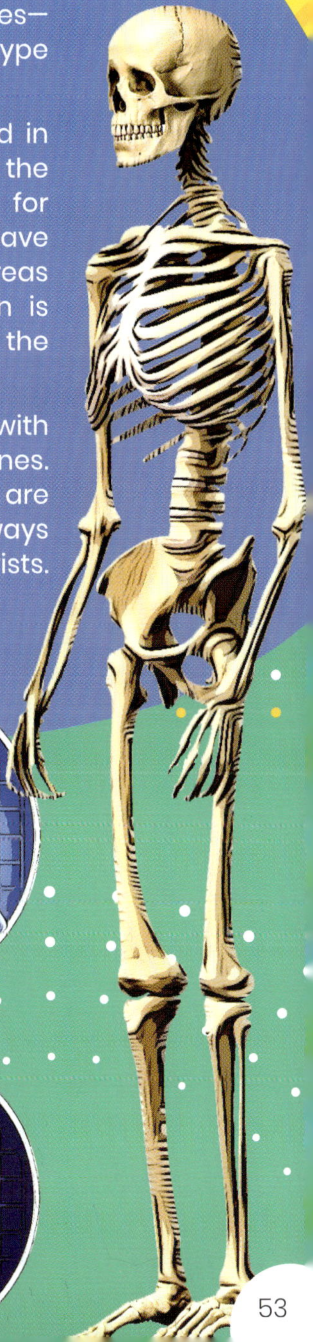

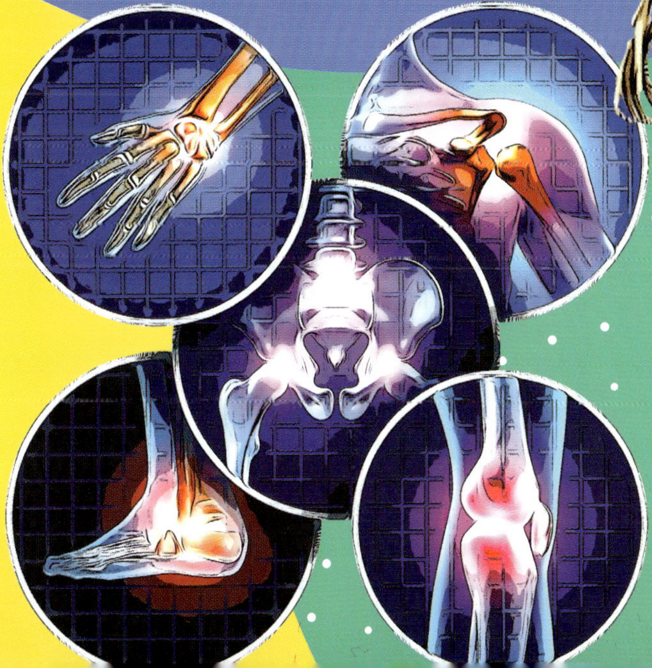

What happens to human bones with age?

Several organs in the body change with age. Obvious changes can be seen in the skin, hair and posture. The changes that are not visible are the ones in the bones, muscles and organs.

Bones, which provide support and structure to the body, start losing bone mass or density as we grow old. This means that the amount of minerals in the bones starts reducing. The spine, which is made up of bones called vertebrae, has a gel-like cushion (called a disc) between each vertebra. As we age, the discs become thinner as they lose water, and the vertebrae lose their minerals and become flatter. And so, the body appears to shrink. The foot arches also become less pronounced, contributing to a slight loss of height.

The long bones in the arms and legs become brittle because of mineral loss, but they do not change length. Joints become stiffer and less flexible. Cartilage may also begin to rub together and show wear and tear. Sometimes, minerals may deposit in and around some joints. This is known as calcification. These changes may lead to inflammation, pain, stiffness and deformity, which affect the posture and walking pattern or gait of a person as they age.

Why do babies have more bones than adults?

New-born babies are born with 305 bones, whereas adults have only 206 bones. A baby's bones grow and change shape every day. When the baby is in the mother's womb, a lot of the bones consist mainly of cartilage, which is softer than actual bone. This allows the baby to move in the womb.

As the baby grows into a toddler, the ends of the bones grow closer together and fuse, thus reducing the number of bones. A baby's skull bones fuse by the age of two. Babies are also born with unfused arm and leg bones, which allow for growth and reduce injury due to falls. When a baby is three years old, knee caps are formed.

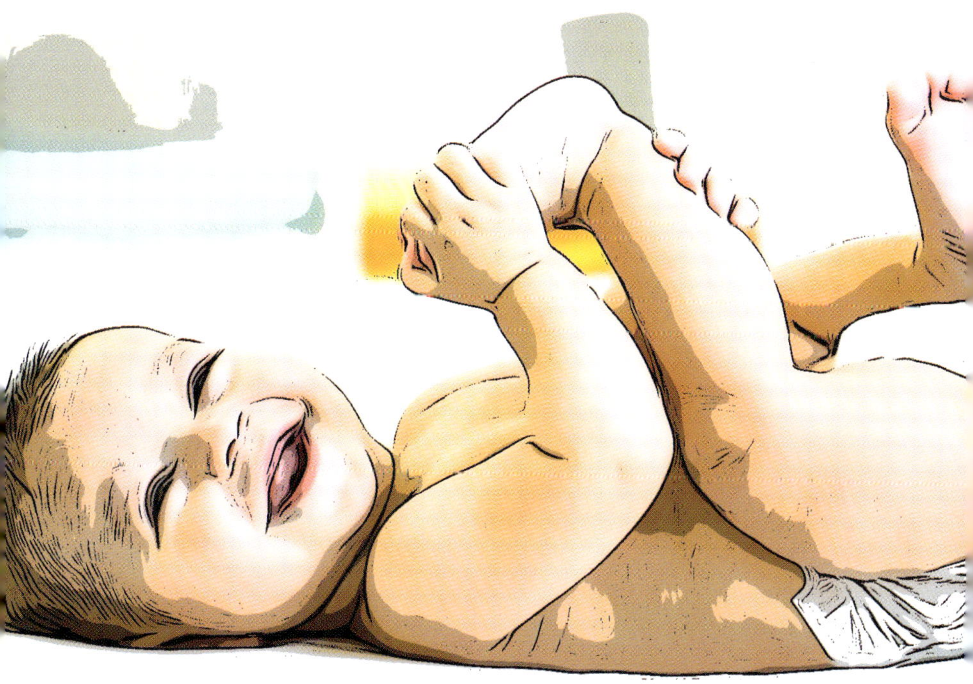

Which are the easiest bones to break?

One of the easiest bones to break is the shoulder bone or clavicle; this is also the most frequently broken bone. The reason this bone can break easily is that unlike other bones in the body, this bone is spongy. The other bone that is easy to snap is the nasal bone, as it is really thin and has little protection. Bones in the fingers and toes are also easy to break and a hard knock on them can cause enough trauma to break them.

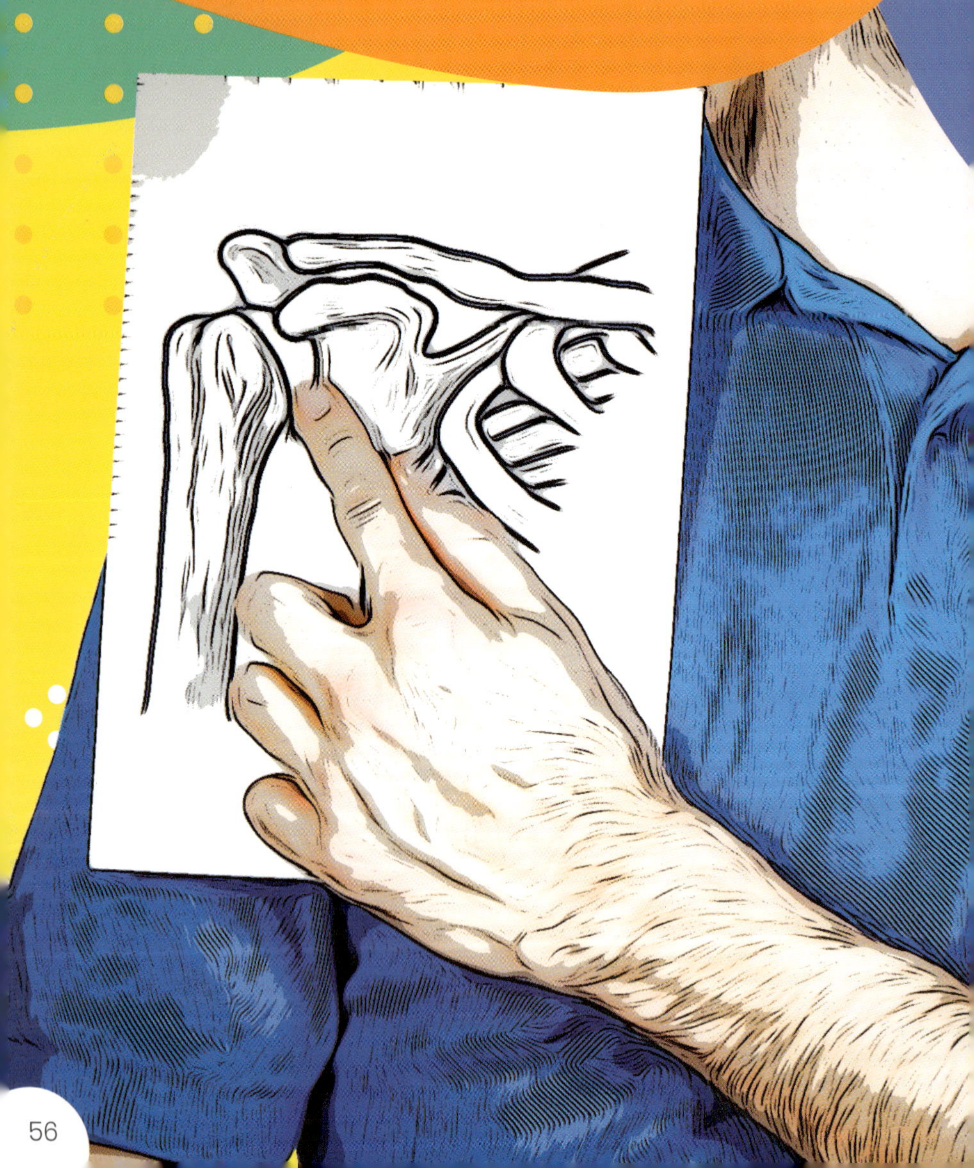

How is it that I am able to bend my elbow?

The human arm has a hinge joint made up of three bones—the humerus, ulna and radius—at the elbow, which enables it to bend in order to perform various functions. Hinge joints are also called ginglymus joints and their main purpose is to allow free movement. Hinge joints are also located in the fingers and knees. They are very similar to hinges that are used on doors so that they can move back and forth. Much like a door hinge, the only movement possible in such joints is extension (opening) and flexion (closing) in one direction.

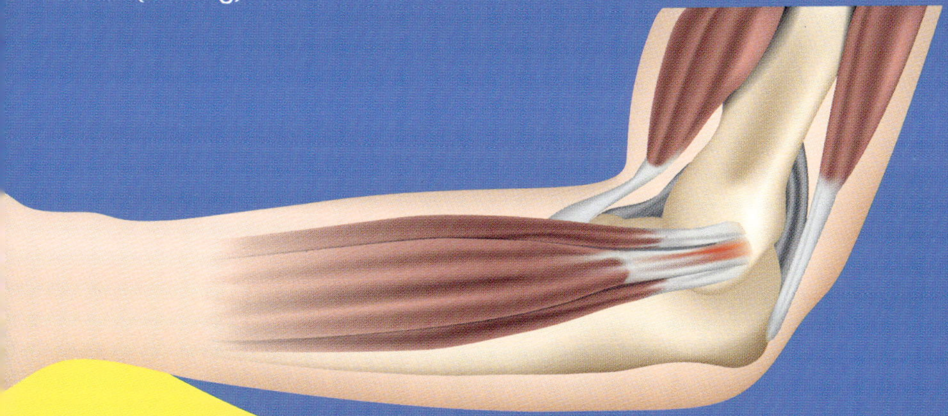

When do bones stop growing?

Bones are constantly changing, either in size or in structure. In babies, bones grow rapidly, and in older people, they may start getting weaker. The basic skeletal structure stops growing at the age of twenty-five, but bones don't stop changing. Bones can become stronger or weaker depending on how they are treated. The muscles around bones can grow with exercise and this can help bones to look bigger. For example, you may have small wrists but forearm exercises will help you develop muscles and make your wrists look bigger.

How do broken bones heal?

Broken bones start to heal from the time they break. Three different cells are responsible for the healing of bones. Osteoblasts, which create bones, and osteoclasts, which reabsorb or dissolve bones, are the two types of cells that work together to shape bones. The third type of cells, chondroblasts, form new cartilage, which help in forming new bone matter.

When a bone breaks, a clot is formed as blood oozes out of blood vessels. This clot helps to stabilize the bone and keeps the two pieces of bone in the right alignment. Without fresh blood, the bone would quickly die. So, the body increases blood supply to the area, which causes swelling. Soon, chondroblasts begin to produce fibre around the broken bone. Next, osteoblasts produce bone cells that form a callus around the bone. The bone now enters the final stage of healing. The blood circulation to the area increases and the bone starts to gain more strength.

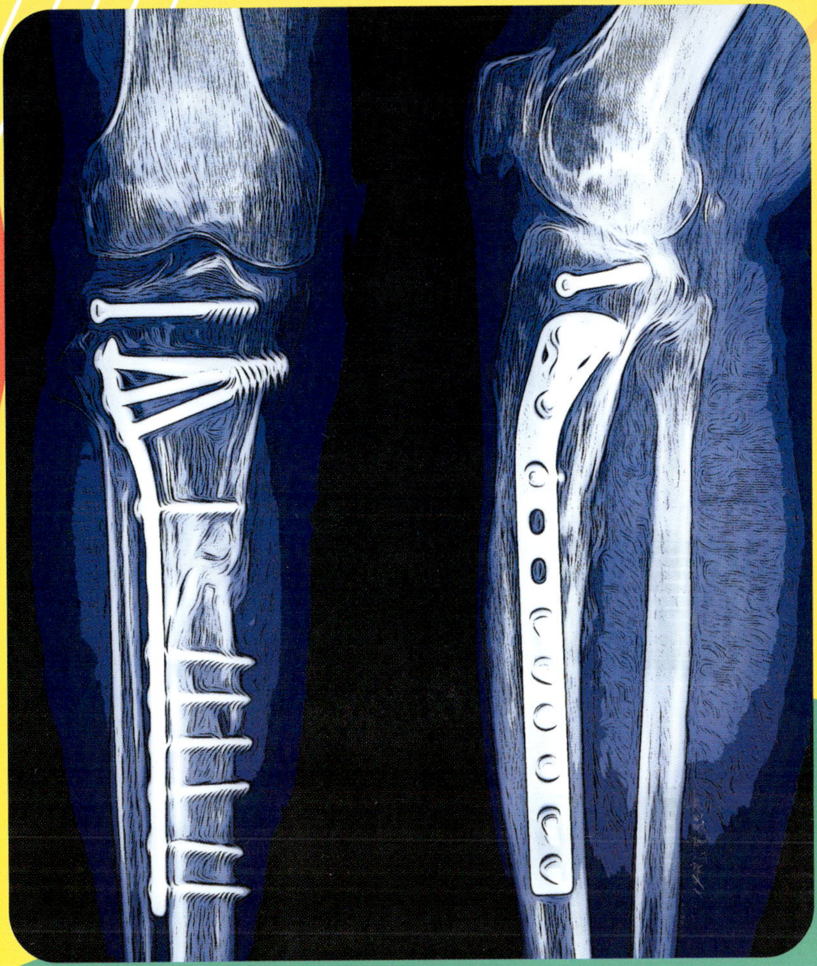

What happens if broken bones don't heal properly?

Sometimes, broken bones do not heal as they are supposed to. This could happen because of wrongly aligned bones, where the broken ends fuse in the wrong place, or broken ends that do not unite because there was too little or too much movement at the site of the fracture.

In such cases, a surgery needs to be done to fix the bone. This could include fixing a metal device called an Ilizarov apparatus that is used to train the bone to heal properly or fixing metal rods when long bones are broken. In some cases, doctors will also use a bone graft, where they transplant tissue from a healthy bone into a broken one to help it mend.

What is bone marrow?

Bone marrow is the spongy tissue inside some of the bones in the body, including the hip and thighbones. It houses a complex network of blood vessels including arteries, veins and capillaries.

Bone marrow is of two types—yellow and red. Yellow bone marrow stores fat, which provides energy to the body. Red bone marrow helps in the production of three types of blood cells, each with a function of its own. These cell types are:

1. Red blood cells or erythrocytes that transport oxygen around the body
2. White blood cells or leukocytes that help fight infection and disease
3. Platelets or thrombocytes that help with clotting after an injury

Bone marrow contains stem cells, which divide constantly to form new cells. Some of the new cells formed continue to remain stem cells while others transform, through a series of stages, to form blood cells. Scientists believe that close to 200 billion new blood cells are formed every day in the human body.

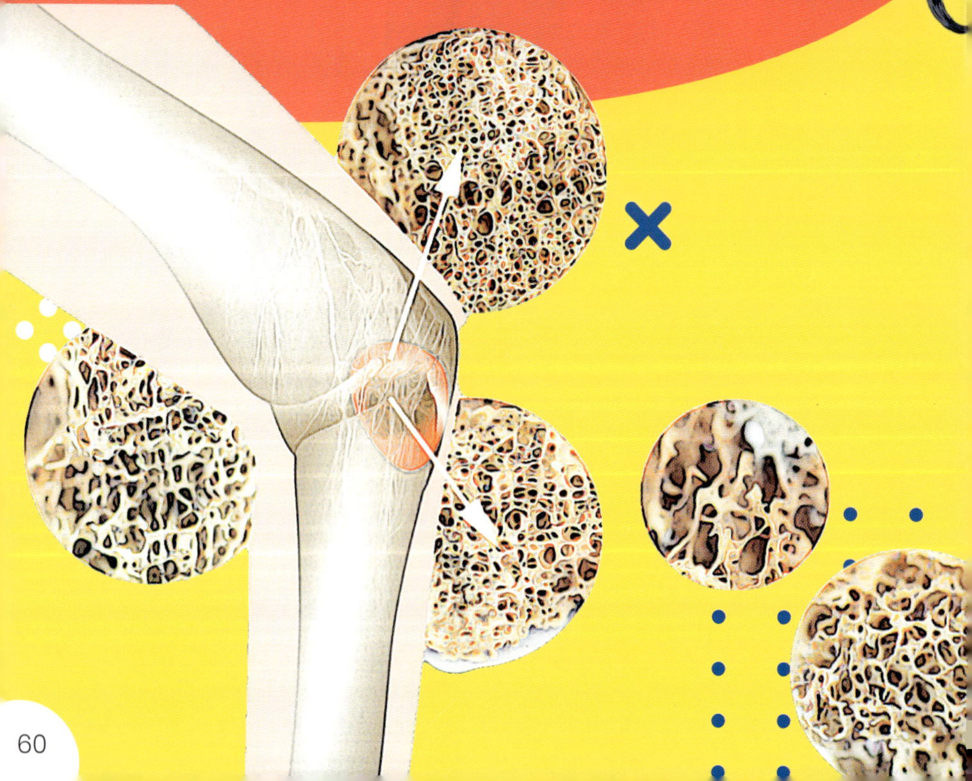

Why do humans have tailbones but no tails?

Humans have evolved from apes that are also tailless. One of the main uses of a tail is to provide balance. It is believed that as evolution progressed and our human ancestors started to walk on two legs, tails disappeared because their function was no longer important.

Yet, humans do have what is known as a vestigial tail, a leftover from the process of evolution. This tail is visible in embryos. By the time a human baby is born, the vestigial tail develops into three to five small bones that can't be seen from the outside. These bones may be fully or partly fused together and are known as the coccyx or tailbone. This tailbone plays a minimal role in our daily lives. It does move slightly as the pelvis, hips and legs move, and it also rotates slightly to support and balance the body. But it has no active role of its own.

What happens to muscles during exercise?

Contrary to popular belief, you do not grow new muscles through exercise. Instead, when you exercise a muscle, more blood flows to it and the muscle cells grow. Each time you feel pain in a muscle, it's actually a tiny tear in the muscle. When the tear heals, the muscle grows stronger and bigger.

Muscle cells or myofibrils are unique. This is because they don't have a single nucleus, but many nuclei. When we work out, the nuclei inside the muscle cells divide to form new cells. This process makes the muscles grow.

Inside each nucleus is a special cellular structure that converts the chemical energy we get from food into the kind of energy our cells can use. These structures fuel the muscles to push harder by giving them more energy. So, the more a muscle develops, so do the nuclei, and thus the muscle has more energy.

Why do people complain of pain while climbing up stairs?

The knee is the meeting point of three major bones—the femur or thigh bone, the tibia or shin bone and the patella or kneecap. These bones work along with muscles and ligaments to allow leg movement and support a person's weight. When the knee bends, the patella slides over the femur. When the cartilage or padding between the bones is in good shape, the bones glide effortlessly over each other. However, if it is damaged, every bending action creates friction between the bones and causes knee pain. Also, at times, legs can hurt while climbing up a flight of stairs because climbing requires energy and tires your body as you lift yourself and climb against gravity.

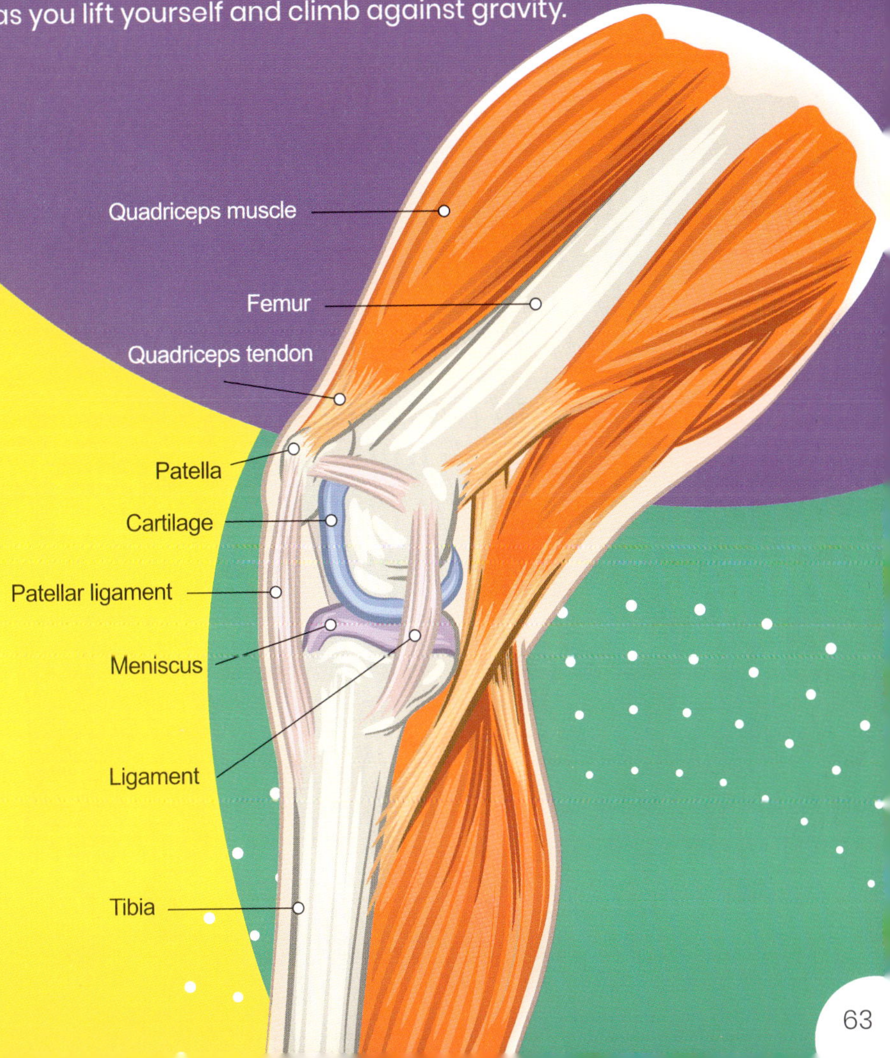

What happens to my body when I run a marathon?

During a marathon, the body makes use of every single type of muscle. This, in turn, uses up a lot of oxygenated blood and almost all the carbohydrate energy supplies stored in the muscles and blood. Once the body has used up this source of energy, it starts using the glycogen deposits from sugars, body fat and proteins to help it fuel the run. The heart is the most used muscle in a marathon. Runners thus need to drink a lot of liquids as this keeps the blood thin and prevents any extra build-up of stress on the kidneys, heart and liver. This also helps the body to cool off faster.

What will happen to my body if it is struck by lightning?

A bolt of lightning generates 3,00,000 volts of energy and courses through the entire body in just 3 milliseconds! Most often, natural lightning will strike the head, shoulders and upper torso. When it does this, it could harm a person fatally.

When a bolt of lightning strikes, it heats up the surrounding air to over 27,000°C, causing third-degree burns at the bolt's entry and exit points. This causes the blood vessels to burst, and creates lightning bolt-shaped burn marks called Lichtenberg figures.

The heat and force with which lightning hits a person will burn and shred clothing and can even blow people out of their shoes. The damage is worse if a person is holding a metal object or wearing metallic objects like chains, necklaces, braces and body piercings. In these cases, the metals also heat up and cause serious burns of their own. A lightning strike can also affect the heart's functioning and cause cardiac arrest.

What physical changes take place in my body when I lie?

Neuroscientists have studied various regions in the brain and concluded that lying is a sign of a sharp and flexible mind. Researchers have also found that the average adult lies about once or twice a day.

Lying emerged soon after languages evolved as it gave humans the ability to get their way without using force. This gave humans many survival benefits during competition for a mate or resources like food. In general, the main reasons for lying include covering up a mistake, avoiding certain situations or people, protecting other people, projecting a better image of oneself or gaining some sort of benefit.

When you lie, you activate the frontal lobe of your brain, which helps suppress the truth. Lying also activates the parts of your brain that are linked to anxiety. The anxiety caused by lying can change your heart rate, breathing pattern and eye movement.

What will happen to my body under anaesthesia?

General anaesthesia is administered either through an injection or a gas that is inhaled. Once anaesthesia is given, you will remain awake for a short period of time before becoming unconscious. During the time you are awake, you will feel lightheaded and most likely confused. You will feel a tingling sensation in your toes and fingertips, and your whole body will begin to feel light, like you are afloat. You will soon start to notice that you cannot feel pain, hear voices or understand what people around you are saying. Your tongue will start to get heavy and then, you will lose consciousness.

There are two other kinds of anaesthesia. Local anaesthesia only numbs small areas; like that given by a dentist to extract a tooth. Regional anaesthesia is when an entire region of the body becomes numb but the patient is awake and conscious, for example, when the lower body of a woman is numbed during the delivery of a baby.

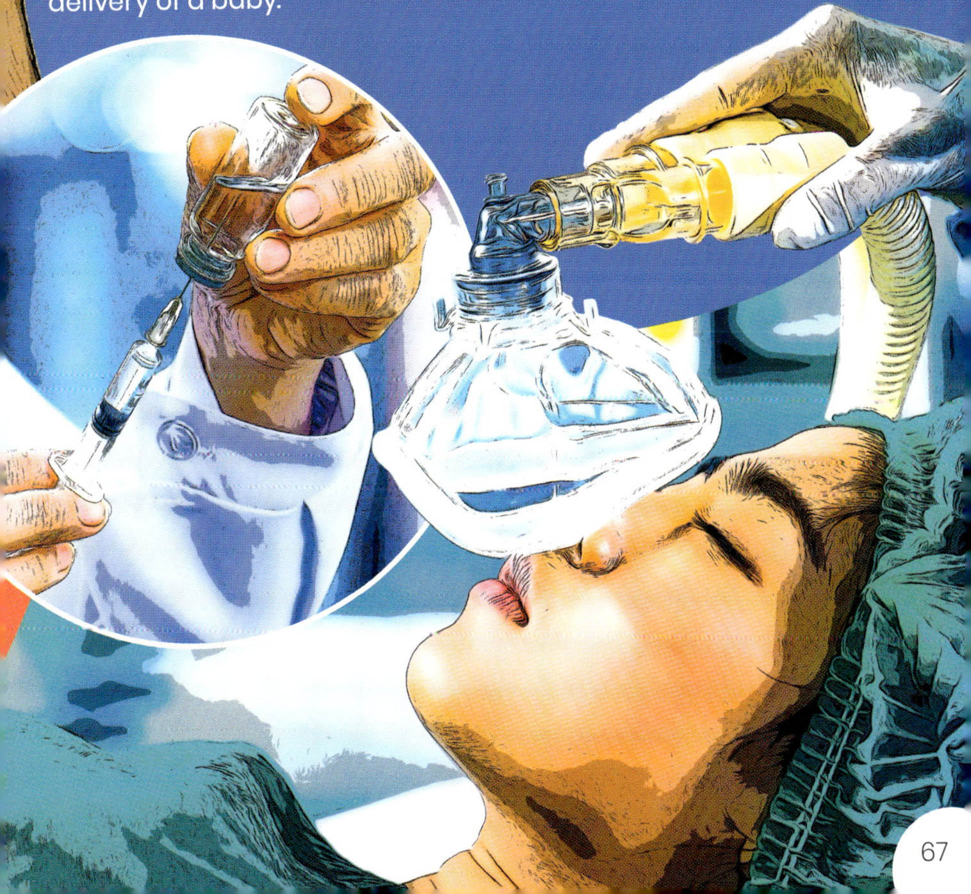

Why are some babies born abnormal?

The physical characteristics of an individual are determined by the chromosomes located inside their cells. Chromosomes are made up of protein and DNA. Every individual is different because their DNA is different.

When a baby is born, it gets half its chromosomes from the mother and the other half from the father. When the two halves combine, new DNA is formed. However, sometimes there are errors in the chromosomes, which prevent the DNA from forming correctly. In such cases, the cells don't have the complete information they need to create a new human being and this results in abnormalities in babies.

Sometimes, accidents or medication taken during pregnancy can also affect the baby when it is growing in the mother's womb and this can lead to abnormalities as well.

What happens to my body during a thirty-minute run?

A number of chemical reactions take place in your body when you perform vigorous exercise.

Your cells start to break down glycogen, which is a form of glucose, to fuel your muscles. The cells also start to absorb glucose directly from the blood. Once the body starts to use the glucose and the muscles start releasing lactic acid, the brain realizes that you are under physical stress. This makes the heart beat faster and direct more blood towards the muscles, away from normal functions that are not in action at that point, like digestion.

What is the difference between breathing and respiration?

Though most people use the words breathing and respiration interchangeably, the two are completely different processes. Breathing is the voluntary physical process of taking in oxygen and giving out carbon dioxide. Respiration is an involuntary physical process wherein the glucose in the food we eat reacts with the oxygen we inhale, breaking it down into simple substances like water, carbon dioxide and energy. The body retains the water and stores the energy, which is used to perform various activities.

Breathing takes place in the lungs through the nose and respiration takes place in cells. While one can physically stop breathing for a few seconds, one cannot stop cell activity, making respiration an involuntary physical process.

Why is it difficult to breathe at higher altitudes?

Air pressure or atmospheric pressure is the weight of the air above a given area on the Earth's surface. In order for a human being to breathe easily, the air pressure outside of the body needs to be higher than inside the body. However, at high altitudes, the air pressure outside is lower than inside the body. Such air is described as thin or rare, and it is difficult for the body to breathe in such air.

Also, at higher altitudes the air gets denser, colder and contains fewer oxygen molecules. This means one needs to take more breaths to get the same amount of oxygen. Most people start to find it difficult to breathe at 5,000 feet above sea level and higher.

What happens to excess protein in the body?

Eating more protein than your body needs can cause more harm than good. Extra protein not only interferes with your health and fitness goals, but also adds to the work the body needs to do to maintain itself. This happens because the body needs to remove all the nitrogen waste that arises from the breakdown of proteins. This can stress out the kidneys and may lead to chronic dehydration.

Extra protein is converted into extra calories and extra sugar, which leads to an increase in fat deposits. Increased blood sugar levels also feed bacterial and yeast infections in the body, aggravating them further.

What happens to donated blood?

Once blood is donated, it is tested to ensure that it doesn't carry any diseases. The clean blood is then properly labelled according to the blood group and transported to a laboratory. Here, the blood may be stored as is or passed through a centrifugation unit to separate it into three essential components–red blood cells, platelets and plasma.

In some cases, the plasma is further processed—depending on the end use of the donated blood—for the treatment of various diseases. Red blood cells and platelets may also be treated further to reduce the possibility of a reaction to blood transfusion in a recipient of the blood.

After processing, the blood components are packaged and stored in large refrigerators and freezers. These are then distributed to hospitals, where they are used for patients in need of a blood transfusion.

What happens in my body when I drink water?

Water instantly refreshes the mind and body. Water eases thirst, which is triggered when the brain detects that the cells in the body are shrinking. The cells are filled with water so the body feels hydrated.

When there isn't enough water in the body, the kidneys start saving water by reducing the amount of urine produced. This means the urine contains more toxins and less water, which makes it darker in colour. Once a person consumes water, the kidneys use the water to throw out unwanted toxins. Water also improves the performance of the brain.

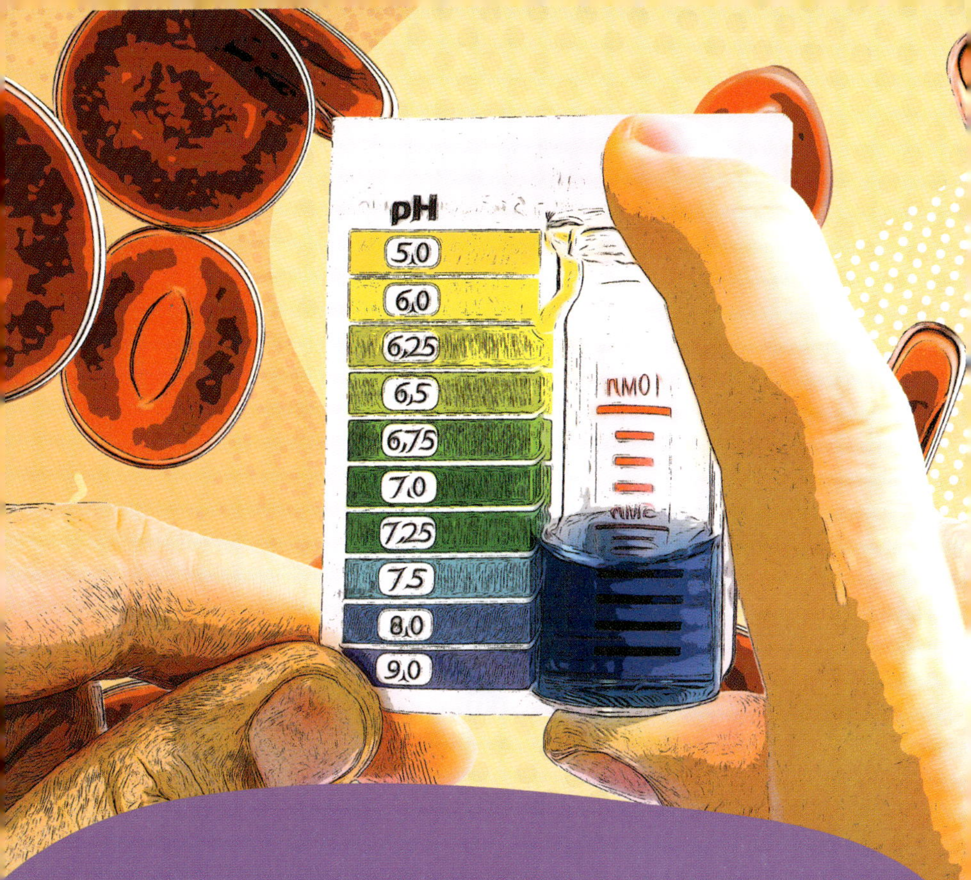

What is the right pH of a healthy body?

pH is the abbreviation for 'potential hydrogen', which is the measure of the concentration of hydrogen ions in a substance. If the pH of a substance is lower than 7, it means that it is rich in hydrogen ions, and if it is higher than 7, it has fewer hydrogen ions. Further, if a substance has a pH ranging from 0 to 6.9, it is described as acidic, and if it has a pH ranging from 7.1 to 14, it is described as alkaline. A substance with a pH of 7 is described as neutral.

The normal pH of healthy human blood is around 7.35 to 7.45, with an ideal pH of 7.4. Anything above or below this figure is an indication of an ailment. If the blood pH moves too far below 6.8 or above 7.8, cells stop functioning. However, the pH within the human body varies greatly. The human digestive tract sees a pH of between 1.5 in the stomach to 8.5 in the lower intestine. These varied pH levels are needed to perform various bodily functions. In general, the body needs to be slightly alkaline in order to be healthy and heal itself.

Why do people get kidney stones?

Kidney stones are hard mineral deposits that can occur in the kidneys. In most cases, they are really small and flush out of the system without causing any harm. But if the stone is big, it can get stuck in the urinary system, causing immense pain. Typically, kidney stones that are smaller than 5 mm are more likely to pass through the urinary system on their own, without requiring medical intervention.

The main job of the kidneys is to convert bodily wastes into urine. Kidney stones are formed when waste products do not get excreted as there isn't enough fluid in the body. Kidney stones are of many types—some are caused due to excessive uric acid in the body, others due to calcium and some due to magnesium and ammonia. The best way to avoid these painful stones is to drink at least three litres of water a day and eat a balanced diet.

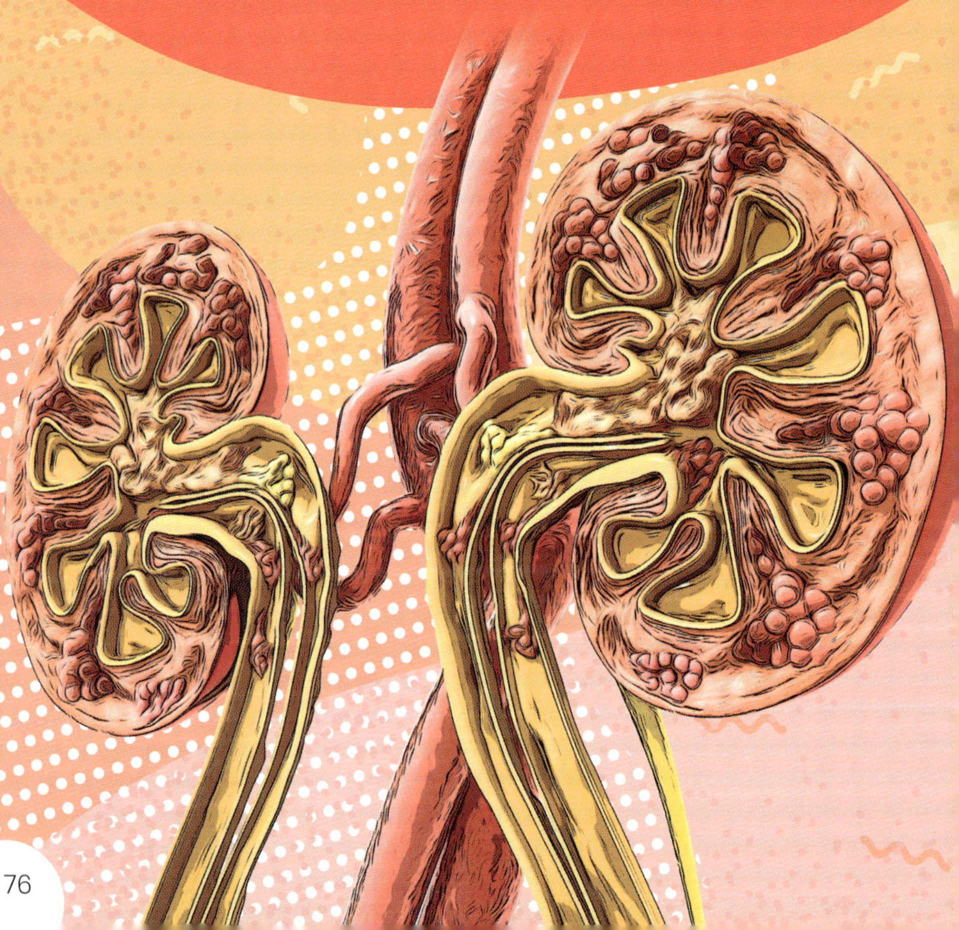

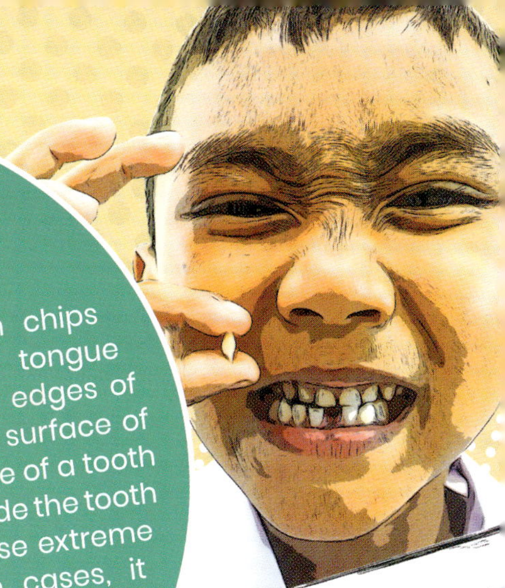

What happens to a tooth when it cracks?

It may not hurt when a tooth chips or breaks. However, when your tongue repeatedly passes over the sharp edges of the broken tooth, it can cause the surface of the tongue to tear. When a big piece of a tooth breaks off or cracks, the nerves inside the tooth may get damaged. This can cause extreme pain and discomfort. In some cases, it may hurt when the tooth is exposed to air or hot and cold foods or drinks. In other cases, the ache can be so intense that it can give you a headache too.

What happens to my teeth when I chew gum?

Chewing gum is an ancient habit. The Greeks chewed mastic, the sap from the mastic tree, while the ancient Mayans of South America favoured chicle, the sap of the sapodilla tree. As you chew gum, more saliva is produced in the mouth. This increased salivary flow helps to neutralize and wash away the acids that are produced when food is broken down in the mouth, thus protecting the teeth.

However, chewing gum that contains sugar can be harmful and increases the chances of developing cavities. Chewing gum may also contain harmful artificial chemicals and colours and shouldn't be eaten very often.

What happens to my body during an electric shock?

When a body gets electrocuted, which happens when it comes in contact with a voltage of around 1 milliamp (mA) or more, the electrons within the source of the electrical energy create an electric current. As the current passes through the body, it comes in contact with the skin and flesh, which act as barriers to the flow. This tension creates heat, which causes burns.

The muscle fibres and neurons get false electric signals, which cause them to react violently. The body is thus thrown away from the source of the current. However, at times, the current can reach the brain. When this happens, it can cause a loss of nervous control, resulting in the loss of consciousness or even death.

What would happen to an unprotected human body in a vacuum?

A vacuum is a space where there is little or no matter. If the human body is exposed to a vacuum, it will immediately start to fall apart. The first visible effect would be the expansion of gases in the lungs and digestive tract. Then, water inside the body would get converted into vapour and moisture in the victim's mouth and eyes would also heat up rapidly. The muscles and soft tissues of the body would see a similar reaction. Thus, parts of the body would swell to twice their usual size. This bloating would result in broken capillaries, which would lead to bruising under the skin. After about 10 seconds, the victim would experience loss of vision and confusion. Within 90 seconds, the blood pressure would fall and the blood would start to boil, leading to heart failure.

Why do we get fevers?

The exact reason for the body developing a fever is still unknown. However, studies by doctors suggest that it is one way for the body to fight diseases. When a foreign body like a virus or bacteria enters the body, the immune system produces white blood corpuscles (WBCs), also known as leucocytes, which fight the infection. The WBCs originate in the bone marrow but travel all across the body. As soon as the number of WBCs increases in the body, it affects the hypothalamus, a region in the brain, and this pushes the body temperature higher. The higher temperature makes it harder for the virus or bacteria to survive. This, in turn, makes it easier for your body to fight the disease.

How does a virus affect the body?

A virus is a tiny living particle that is so small that it cannot be seen by the naked eye. Viruses cause illnesses in human beings when they enter the body and start multiplying rapidly. When this happens, we may develop a fever, cough, cold or other infections.

Viruses spread from one person to another if one does not follow healthy habits like washing one's hands and covering the mouth when one coughs or sneezes. Since viruses spread by contact, a person can also catch a virus if they touch something contaminated and then touch their nose, mouth or eyes without washing their hands. The chances of catching most viruses by breathing them in are quite low.

Viruses can cause various ailments. One such ailment is swine flu, a respiratory illness of pigs, which can at times affect humans. Another is the Zika virus, which can live in human blood for up to a week. During this time, the virus can also pass from mothers to their unborn babies, resulting in babies being born with deformed brains. More recently, the virus SARS-CoV-2 has caused the coronavirus pandemic, which has made millions of people ill around the world.

What happens to the human body if it doesn't get enough sleep?

The body uses sleep time to repair and improve the immune system and for growth, while the brain uses this time to sort through and store information. When the body doesn't get enough sleep, a person feels tired and cranky and is not able to think clearly. Brain functions like memory, decision-making, reasoning and problem-solving start to worsen if one doesn't get at least seven hours of sleep. Moreover, the brain fails to store information about new things and thus, one is unable to make new memories and learn new things.

Lack of sleep can also affect the immune system, which fights against ailments, the respiratory system and the skeletal system, thereby affecting the bones and muscles too. In children, lack of sleep can result in nightmares or sleep terrors. Nightmares are dreams that can be scary and sleep terrors are often described as extreme nightmares. Therefore, it is necessary for children to get at least ten hours of sleep.

Why do I get sweaty palms when I am nervous?

The medical condition for sweaty palms is known as palmar hyperhidrosis. However, not everyone suffers from sweaty palms. According to researchers, only three per cent of the population suffers from this condition and its effects stay the same in every season, including winter.

Palmar hyperhidrosis is usually triggered by stressful situations. In case of fear, excitement or nervousness, a sweat gland in the palm of the hand is stimulated. This occurs because of increased activity in the sympathetic nervous system, which controls one's response to stressful situations, as well as an increase in the hormone epinephrine, which is released from the adrenal gland that lies on top of the kidneys.

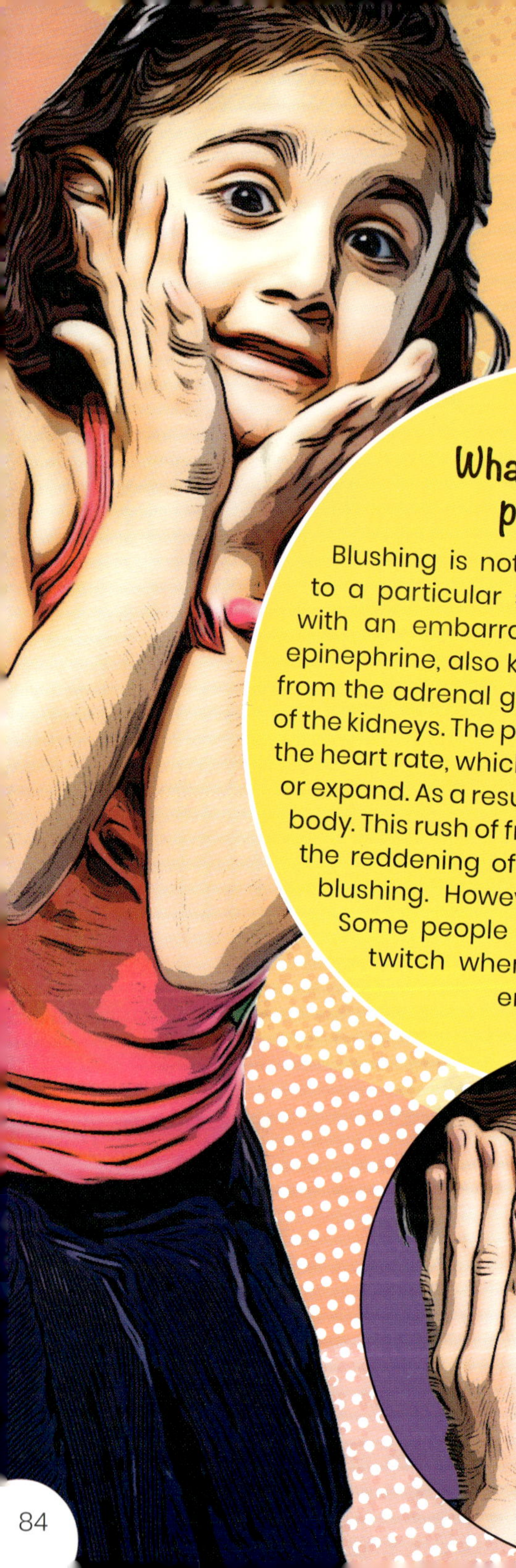

What happens when people blush?

Blushing is nothing but a way of reacting to a particular situation. When one is faced with an embarrassing situation, the hormone epinephrine, also known as adrenaline, is released from the adrenal glands, which are located on top of the kidneys. The presence of adrenaline speeds up the heart rate, which makes the blood vessels dilate or expand. As a result, more blood is supplied to the body. This rush of fresh oxygen-rich blood causes the reddening of the skin, which is known as blushing. However, not everyone blushes. Some people may tap their fingers or twitch when they are nervous or embarrassed.

What happens to my body when I cry?

Extreme reactions like sadness, fear, anger, stress and even happiness can bring tears to a person's eyes. The amygdala in the brain is responsible for processing a person's emotions. This organ sends a signal to the hypothalamus, another part of the brain, which in turn sends a message to the lacrimal or tear glands, causing one to cry. When one cries, the vocal cords in the throat also swell up, creating tightness in the throat.

Scientists have proved that different emotions bring about different kinds of tears. Tears are infused with chemicals called endorphins, which calm a person down. Tears also blur sight, making a person less aggressive.

What happens to people when they get angry?

When a person gets angry, there is a definite change in the heart rate, tension in the arteries and production of certain hormones. The left side of the brain also becomes more stimulated. Various people show different physiological changes when they get angry. Some people start shaking while others display facial twitching, reddening of the skin colour and, sometimes, even crying. All these changes are exhibited because of hormonal and emotional changes that lead to a physiological change in the body.

What happens to my body when I am scared?

Fear is your body's response to a likely threat. When your body detects something around you that could harm you, the adrenal glands release a hormone called adrenaline. This hormone has several effects on different parts of your body. Your heart rate increases, which causes the blood to circulate faster and deliver extra oxygen to the body's muscles. You also breathe faster and deeper to take in more oxygen. When the muscles are oversaturated with oxygen, they move faster and help you make a quick escape from the source of danger.

Another effect of adrenaline is the dilation of pupils, which allows more light to enter your eyes and helps you identify the source of threat faster. This helps you find quick and safe escape routes. Adrenaline also stimulates the cells in the liver to convert glycogen to glucose, which is required to meet the energy levels required during an escape.

GLOSSARY

Abdomen: the lower part of the body that contains most of the digestive system as well as other important organs like the liver

Amnesia: loss of memory which could be temporary or permanent

Artery: blood vessels that carry oxygen-rich blood from the heart to other parts of the body

Atria: the two upper chambers of the human heart from where blood enters the lower chambers or ventricles

Blood Group: the classification of blood based on the presence of substances called antigens, which stimulate the body's immune system to react, and antibodies, which attack harmful bacteria and viruses

Blood Pressure: a measure of the force with which the heart pumps blood across the body

Blood Transfusion: the process of transferring blood or blood products into the blood stream through a vein

Blood Vessel: a tubular structure that transports blood across the body

Bone Mass: a measure of the amount of minerals like calcium and potassium found in bones, which is used to analyse how strong the bones are

Capillary: the smallest type of blood vessel in the body

Cartilage: a strong supporting and connecting tissue found in human joints and the nose, throat and ears

Cell: the smallest biological unit in a living being; the basic building block that forms tissues and organs

Cerebral Cortex: the wrinkly outer or top covering over both the hemispheres of the brain

Chromosomes: thread-like structures present within the nucleus of a cell that contain DNA and are passed on from parent to child

Circulatory System: an organ system that consists of the heart, blood vessels, blood, lymphatic vessels and glands and is responsible for the movement of blood across the body

Congenital: a medical condition or disease present from birth

Cornea: the transparent covering on the front part of the eye that allows light to enter the eye

Diaphragm: a muscular layer between the lungs and stomach that plays an important role in controlling breathing

DNA: full form: deoxyribonucleic acid; a molecule that contains all the instructions needed for an organism to develop, live and reproduce

Embryo: an unborn baby in the early stages of development

Enzyme: molecules like proteins that speed up chemical reactions that take place within cells

Epidermis: the thin, waterproof outer layer of the skin which protects everything that lies under it

Eustachian Tube: a canal that connects the middle ear to the upper throat and back of the nasal cavity

Follicle: a small sac that secretes a fluid or a sac from which something grows, like a hair follicle

Frontal Lobe: the front part of the brain that is responsible for problem solving, memory, language, judgement and emotional expression

Gene: a unit of genetic information that is present on a chromosome and is transferred from parent to child

Grey Matter: a major component of the brain that is full of nerve cells called neurons

Gland: an organ that produces and releases substances that perform specific functions, for example the salivary gland produces saliva

Hormones: chemicals produced by certain glands that affect different processes in the body

Hypothalamus: a part of the brain that plays a vital role in releasing hormones and regulating body temperature

Immune System: a complex system of proteins and cells that fight infections in the body

Iris: a thin structure in the eye that determines eye colour and controls the size of the pupil, thus determining how much light enters the eye

Ligament: an extremely strong strip of tissue that connects bones, limits movement, supports organs and keeps them in position

Melanin: a natural pigment found in the skin, hair and eyes that determines their colour

Neurons: cells that are basic working units of the brain and send information to other cells in the body

Nucleus: a structure found inside a cell that is surrounded by a membrane and contains all the genetic material of the cell

Olfactory: related to the sense of smell

Parietal Lobe: the part of the brain that is placed towards the centre and is responsible for interpreting sensations

Plasma: the yellowish liquid part of blood that carries water, salts and enzymes

Platelets: tiny cells that circulate in the blood and help in clotting; they are also called thrombocytes

Pregnancy: the time period during which one or more babies develop in the womb of a female

Puberty: the physical changes that take place in a child's body as he/ she matures into a young adult

Pus: a thick, yellow or greenish coloured liquid that oozes out of infected tissue or wounds

Receptors: cells or groups of cells that receive stimuli like touch or information that comes from chemicals in the body

Red Blood Cell: a type of blood cell that is made in the bone marrow; also called a red blood corpuscle or erythrocyte

Reproduce: to produce a new living being

Resting Heart Rate: the number of times the heart beats per minute while at complete rest; it is an indicator of one's physical fitness

Short Term Memory: information that is retained by the brain for use over a short period of time

Stem Cell: unique cells that have the ability to develop into specialized cell types

Sympathetic Nervous System: a part of the nervous system that activates specific responses in the body, like sweating to cool off

Tendon: a strong band of tissue that connects a muscle to a bone

Tissue: groups of cells that come together based on their structure and function, for example muscle tissues

Vein: blood vessels that carry deoxygenated blood from all over the body to the heart

Ventricles: two large muscular chambers present towards the bottom of the human heart

ABOUT

ROBINAGE

INDIA'S FAVOURITE NEWSPAPER FOR CHILDREN

Founded in 2008, *RobinAge* has won multiple national and international awards, including three Parents' Choice Awards (USA). It is read by children aged between four and fifteen years and reaches schools and children's homes across India via subscription.

RobinAge carries news and information on current affairs, science, history, sports, careers, culture and environment along with activities, puzzles and interactive projects.

Each fortnightly issue also includes two supplements—an Activity Sheet that makes the newspaper's content interactive and a special Jr RobinAge for our younger readers, which includes fun activities, general knowledge and the Each One Teach One Programme, which children can use to learn and teach basic English.

To learn more about *RobinAge,* visit www.robinage.com